What's wrong with ... Financial Advice UK?

Written and published by Alistair MacDougall 2025

Copyright © Alistair MacDougall 2025

All rights reserved

CONTENTS

FOREWORD 5
INTRODUCTION 13
CHAPTER 1 – ISSUE NUMBER FIVE ...
CULTURE 17
CHAPTER 2 – ISSUE NUMBER FOUR ... VAT .. 39
CHAPTER 3 – ISSUE NUMBER THREE ...
PENSION TRANSFERS 59
CHAPTER 4 – ISSUE NUMBER TWO ...
SWITCHING 133
CHAPTER 5 - ISSUE NUMBER ONE
...ONGOING ADVICE 169

FOREWORD

I retired in January 2024, having worked for 51 years in financial services.

Most of that time was one or more of:

- Enjoyable
- Interesting
- Challenging
- Frustrating
- All of the above
- But mostly the first two!

Over the years, I've been fortunate to work with many individuals I admired or who inspired unconditionally. Inevitably, I have also crossed paths with people in financial services who merited little admiration and who only inspired me to continue making whatever contribution I could to challenging and changing poor practice, particularly in the advice sector, long after I should have sailed off into the retirement sunset, happily ticking off my personal bucket list.

This modest little book was one of my bucket list items. It has taken me a bit longer to finalise than I had hoped. The reasons for that will become clearer toward the end of this foreword.

The content is aimed at the financial advice sector generally. Advisers and firms that do good quality work should find reassuring confirmation of that. My hope is that other firms and individual advisers will be sufficiently open minded to read what follows and perhaps recognise some aspects of the way they currently work that would benefit from a rethink.

The chapters are built around what I believe are some hard truths that advisers might care to reflect upon and use as a basis for change of practice and/or mind set. The list is in 'reverse order' of risk to advice firms and advisers, such that the last chapter outlines what I believe is the biggest threat - and possibly the most difficult to resolve.

Armed with that detail, you might be tempted to jump straight to chapter five. Well, you've bought the book so you can do that if you want to – but if you do, you'll miss the chance to spot other issues that I believe cry out for recognition and which could be minimised or avoided with the right response.

I am pretty certain that many of the firms and individuals that form my 'target market' won't ever read this. I can't do anything about that other than bring horses and water to mind. However, as you are reading this, I am thankful – though not for reasons of personal profit, see below*.

I recognise that the content is not likely to gain me a multitude of new friends. I'm fine with that. All I ask is that people read this book with an "if the cap fits approach". By definition of its primary purpose, i.e. drawing attention to issues in the UK financial advice world, the content might well come across as hypercritical of the advice sector. That is the intention. Everyone likes to receive positive feedback so I could simply have written about all the good firms and advisers I have come across and all the great advice and help they've provided to their clients over the years – a self-congratulatory exhortation to 'keep up the good work'. But that would be ultimately pointless. My intention is to try to highlight things in the advice sector that I believe require attention. If you truly believe that not one iota of the issues raised apply to you then you can surely give yourself a virtual gold star. And I am happy to repeat that I know of many quality advisers and firms. Good firms are definitely out there.

On the other hand, many firms operate with poor practices. In my experience this is rarely a deliberate choice. The poor practice usually stems from a perpetuation of old bad habits learned in a previous firm/network/bank, or poor management, or poor internal or external compliance advice. Regrettably there are also all too many examples of firms or advisers that implement poor practices, whether knowingly or unknowingly, because of the temptation of low hanging fruit and a shortcut to easy revenue. Some of the poorest/riskiest practices I have come across are included in the chapters of this book. If any of the issues included hit close to home, it will be reasonable to conclude that there is remedial work to be done.

The important thing is to maintain an open mind. You might agree with the points made, or you might take part or total issue. Either way is fine by me – I can only reiterate that this book comprises my honest observations based upon a long career around all aspects of the UK financial advice sector and I hope that you might find some of what I write here to be at least thought provoking.

* *Cancer Research UK*

I have no desire for a sympathy vote but a major driver for my decision to finally retire and also to create this book was a problem with my health. I was diagnosed with angiosarcoma in 2021 which required some radical facial surgery. Not very pleasant as you can imagine. And the heavy bandaging during the six to eight-week recovery period made me feel like I was playing the lead in Phantom of the Opera. I don't even like musicals!

The cancer recurred in 2022 and I underwent the same surgery all over again followed by six weeks of daily radiotherapy involving my head being entombed in a custom moulded close fitting Perspex face mask and bolted to a hard surface. Did I mention I am extremely claustrophobic? That was followed by "Oh, and stay out of the sunlight for twelve months."

Regular checks showed that I remained free of this rare and aggressive cancer for two years and I was looking forward to 2024, retirement and lots of ticking off from a long deferred bucket list. It was not to be. Unfortunately, the cancer recurred for a second time in March 2024. Having spread to my lungs, the only treatment option was chemotherapy which proceeded while I was working on this book. Hence the book has taken a bit longer to finish than I had anticipated back in January when I retired. Regular hospital visits, tests and chemo sessions, coupled with general daily fatigue resulted in a lot of potential writing time being 'lost'. On the upside, some time has been saved. For example, the chemo drug I received led to a rapid loss of hair, in particular head and facial hair, so saving time in monthly haircuts and daily shaving. Talk about a close shave. Chemo, the best a man can get!

The book is intended as my parting contribution to the advice sector following a lifetime of working in and around the sector. It is not intended for any personal profit. I have set the price to the minimum allowed by Amazon which is intended to ensure that the printing costs and royalty payments are covered. I have also set the royalty level at the minimum allowed and will be donating the net royalties to Cancer Research UK.

I have set up a Just Giving page and hope that you might consider a donation to Cancer Research UK. My thanks in advance if you do donate. Remember to Gift Aid your donation if possible. The page is here:

https://www.justgiving.com/page/alistair-macdougall-1735923728012

If you get an error with this link, or are reading the print version of the book and don't want to type all that in, go to the Just Giving home page at ...

https://www.justgiving.com/

... and search for Alistair MacDougall. In the event that the page is closed by the time you get around to reading this, a donation directly to Cancer Research UK is always possible!

It would be great if you could help me reach a few more people so please feel free to recommend, or at least mention, the book to others who might be interested in the content of this book. I don't even mind if you lend them your copy to read so long as you ask them to consider making a donation! I would also be grateful if you want to share the link with any friends or colleagues, even if they would have no interest in reading the book. Thank you.

INTRODUCTION

In the foreword, I mentioned that the 'Issues' in this book are covered in reverse order, in increasing order of risk as I see it, with the biggest issue being covered in chapter five. Here is a brief overview of what is covered in each chapter – in reverse order.

Chapter five – Ongoing advice

What I believe to be the biggest unrecognised and unaddressed issue for firms – potentially an existential threat for many firms. This chapter explores the three risk aspects ...

1. The charging model
2. The delivery
3. The default

... and what action firms need to take.

Chapter four – Switching

Switching products held by newly acquired clients seems to be pretty much a default position in adviser firms. That is a major issue in itself. But the way that many firms provide switching advice has long been less than satisfactory. Chapter four examines the underlying reasons and remedies.

Chapter three – Pension Transfers

This chapter probably needs no introduction! There cannot be any adviser that is unaware of the debacle that has been the provision of unsuitable pension transfer advice by many firms since the Pension Freedoms arrived in April 2015 – nor the significant client harm that resulted. Unfortunately, both for the advice sector and the many clients who suffered from unsuitable advice, the damage is largely done and cannot be undone. This chapter looks at the background to the problem and identifies the causes. But chapter three is not merely a sad story of poor advice. The issues and problems identified have relevance to all advice. Highlighting those may provide a clear route to how the quality of financial advice generally can be improved.

Chapter two – VAT

In my experience, VAT on adviser charges is a topic that remains poorly understood and largely ignored. Most firms probably looked at the various articles and provider guides (I wrote one of the guides) that were prevalent around RDR time, decided that VAT did not apply to what they do and have not thought about it since. The problem is that what many firms do and how they go about it has changed since those heady early days following RDR. Some of what firms currently do could well be subject to VAT.

Firms might immediately think that's OK. "We're not registered for VAT so we do not need to charge it." But the question that follows is "How will you know if or when the firm needs to register – or if it should already be?".

That involves firms having a process to identify revenue from exempt services and potentially VATable services. And that requires an adequate knowledge of how VAT applies in the context of financial advice and related services.

Chapter two provides an overview of key points relating to VAT and financial services and indicates some of the potential issues and the action that firms should be considering.

Chapter one – Culture

And so we come to chapter one. This chapter is not about any single issue. Indeed, some readers might not agree that any or all of what is covered here are issues at all. That's fine. The topics covered are miscellaneous personal observations which, for want of any better label, I have decided are all loosely related to the culture of the advice sector. Right or wrong, that is how I see them.

CHAPTER 1 – ISSUE NUMBER FIVE … CULTURE

CHAPTER 1 – ISSUE NUMBER FIVE ...

... CULTURE

The personal observations in this chapter are in no particular order.

Life or death?

I have often thought that advisers do not always seem to recognise the seriousness of the job. There may be a subconscious feeling that it's not a life or death situation. The underlying thought process may be that of course there are jobs that carry clear potentially fatal consequences – surgeons, military, emergency services and the like - but financial advice is not one of them. I disagree.

While not strictly life or death, providing unsuitable advice can be seriously life changing for clients. This was hammered home to me some years ago when I met with a client in his early eighties who had received some seriously bad investment advice from a bank adviser. As a consequence, he had lost a substantial proportion of his investment. The money he had invested was the result of hard work and saving since leaving school at age fourteen and was intended to sustain his rather modest needs in retirement. The losses, caused in no small part by charges and penalties, meant that his retirement plans became borderline non-viable and he was at severe risk of running out of money. How he described his feelings always stayed with me over the years – *"What the adviser did not seem to recognise is that it took me a lifetime to make that money and I will never have another chance to make it again."*

Or consider the pension transfer debacle (examined further in chapter three) … so many people have been placed in a position where they may not have sufficient funds to meet their lifetime needs.

Or clients where advisers pick at the low hanging fruit of pension transfers, switching existing investments or investing new money – yet do not address, for example, the client's protection or IHT planning needs. That could result in a significantly detrimental situation when the client dies.

So providing financial advice may not be life or death, but it's close.

Clients are people too

The sad tale of the elderly client mentioned in the 'Life or Death' section is a good example of something else too. Every time I come across examples of poor advice like that, which unfortunately has been often, makes me wonder if the adviser saw the client as a person, or merely as a source of income. That the latter mindset may well not be a rarity is perhaps confirmed by the regular online headlines around acquisitions. Typically, the headline to these articles is along the lines of "A buys B and increases AUM by £Xm." No mention of the adviser team that is being taken on and definitely no mention of the quality or quantity of clients being 'acquired'. It's like there are no people involved in the transaction, only £Xm!

Self-awareness?

How do advisers see themselves? That's a big question. A succinct answer might be 'as a profession'.

For years, and certainly since the RDR's increased qualification requirements, there have been regular calls for financial advice to be considered a profession without, it seems to me, much in the way of agreement as to what that actually means. There are many dictionary definitions but not a lot of commonality between them. The closest relevant definition I can find is along the lines of ...

'a profession is a group of individuals who adhere to ethical standards and who hold themselves out as, and are accepted by the public as, possessing special knowledge and skills derived from education and training at a high level'

That could be argued to be a fair description of a financial adviser. But does it make financial advice a profession? Well, there are definitely educational and training standards in play but describing a level four qualification as high-level education is perhaps a bit of a stretch. It is generally accepted to be equivalent to the level of the qualifications listed below ...

- certificate of higher education (CertHE)

- higher apprenticeship
- higher national certificate (HNC)
- level 4 NVQ

And regrettably, history clearly shows that a significant proportion of advisers have not adhered to the required ethical and regulatory standards over the years, hence the various well-known mis-selling events and the fact that the FOS and FSCS need to exist. I think it unlikely that the long list of firms/advisers that have been sanctioned or even banned by the regulator does not include a fair smattering of Chartered Firms, New Model Advisers and individuals with 'higher' level qualifications (e.g. pension transfer specialist).

It is of interest that the UK Government publishes a list of 'regulated professions and their regulators' here:

https://www.gov.uk/government/publications/professions-regulated-by-law-in-the-uk-and-their-regulators/uk-regulated-professions-and-their-regulators#list-of-uk-regulated-professions-and-their-regulators

The sizeable list includes obvious professions such as teachers, solicitors, nurses and various other medical related disciplines. It also includes some rather less obvious entries - Road/Street Works Operative, Door Supervisor, Security Guard and Waste Manager.

Notably, it does not include Financial Advisers in any shape or form!

Then there is the Financial Adviser versus Financial Planner debate. Despite loud declarations to the contrary, this is a distinction without a difference in my humble opinion. Different label but fundamentally the same job.

Beyond the mundane level of financial advisers/planners lie the exalted ranks of life coaches and well-being 'experts'. Now, it seems to me that there are clearly individuals who by qualification and experience can help people needing assistance with the vagaries and difficulties of life but I don't personally believe that working as a financial adviser inherently imbues any credible degree of competence to offer a life coaching service. Call me old fashioned, but I think it would be best all round if financial advisers just 'stick to their knitting' and provide financial advice competently and compliantly. I would not expect to obtain that sort of specialist personal coaching support from a lawyer or accountant or a Road/Street Works Operative, nor would I trust it if offered. The 'each to his own' principle should apply. People that need a leaky tap fixing find a plumber. People that need financial advice find a financial adviser. And so on!

Pavlovian response

Many readers may be aware of the experiments of Ivan Pavlov who, in the late 1800s found that he could condition dogs to associate red meat with particular sounds. The dogs soon started to salivate when they heard the sound, without any meat being present at all.

Although slightly less prevalent recently, there was a lengthy period post-RDR when adviser comments posted in response to certain online articles always seemed to evoke a similar boringly predictable Pavlovian reaction.

The trigger articles were usually about one of three things – the FCA, SJP and Complaints Firms (CMCs).

The comments tended to follow similar lines each time:

- **The FCA**
  "the FCA is useless" "another case of closing the door after the horse has bolted"
- **SJP**
  "Dear Editor, stop referring to SJP as successful national advisers – they are a slick money grabbing marketing organisation that charges too much"
- **Complaints Firms**
  These tended to attract the harshest vitriol.
  "Shysters" "Fraudsters" "they know if they throw enough mud at companies some of it will stick, their clients will get a pay-out and they can skim some of the cream off the top" "ambulance chasers" "no win no fee merchants"

The comments always struck me as having a common underlying tone – grievance.

The FCA comments suggested a feeling of poor financial advisers who would be better off if only the FCA would leave them alone. Too many regulations, too much cost. *"Why doesn't the FCA go and stop all these scams that go on?"* The last comment being reminiscent of what police often hear when they stop a speeding driver, "Have you nothing better to do? Why don't you go and arrest some real criminals?"

The SJP comments hinted at a combination of 'hard done by' and envy. "How come SJP always get away with <whatever the current topic is>?" Like it or not (and

25

advisers generally seem to vote for 'not'), SJP have undoubtedly been financially successful over the years, leading to some advisers seeing the firm through green tinged glasses.

As advisers were the target at which complaints companies directed fire, it is entirely understandable that advisers considered them as 'the enemy'. But the criticisms tended to be emotive and ad hominem in nature rather than being based around cogent arguments. Hence 'shyster' etc. In addition to the absence of any carefully considered points, there never seemed to be any recognition of the reality that advisers actually did (and do) sometimes give poor advice, resulting in financial detriment to clients. Many of those clients would have consulted the adviser in the first place because they did not feel they had enough knowledge to navigate their way through investment and tax minefields. So it should be no surprise, nor considered a bad thing, that those clients then take the option of some assistance when they feel that they have something to complain about. After all, one of the primary reasons we have financial regulations at all is because the market is asymmetric. In written evidence to Parliament, the FCA stated,

"Just about all consumer legislation seeks to do one thing; to even up the negotiating positions of buyers and sellers. This is true in financial services as well. Most financial regulation has been put in place to try to overcome the knowledge asymmetry that exists between buyers and sellers of financial products. The seller knows all there is

to know about the product, the buyer knows very little, apart from the advertising hype and, if they have read and understood them, the restrictions and conditions in the contract."

Now, I have seen many factory-line, formulaic and opportunistic complaints put forward by complaints firms. So, I am certainly not aiming to provide a blanket defence for them here. However, it should be acknowledged that, since they came under the remit of FCA regulation in 2019, excessive and unfair charging and other poor practices have been under the cosh and many firms have been forced out. And it has to be recognised that not all complaints raised through complaints firms are without merit. There is no ambulance to chase unless there is a patient!

Finally, the comments that always struck me as being pure irony were those that sought to denigrate the complaints firms based around the 'no win, no fee' business model. The implication being that this method of charging clients is somehow beyond the pale. The irony comes from the fact that most advisers did, and still do, charge clients for advice on exactly the same business model – a contingent percentage-based fee! The adviser's constant blind spot! There is more on this in Chapter five.

Advice gap

Is the advice gap really a sales gap? In my experience, advisers often take umbrage at any suggestion they sell product as much as they provide advice. The 'sell' word perhaps being another Pavlov trigger.

However, having been around the world of financial advice since well before the first regulations came in, never mind the much later Retail Distribution Review (RDR), I can readily contrast the much vaunted 'advice gap' against the reality that existed pre-RDR. The implications of discussions around the advice gap are that it was caused by the RDR and did not exist pre-RDR. This does not bear close scrutiny.

In those pre-RDR commission paying days, many consumers were sold investments that were selected by the 'adviser' for a variety of reasons, many of which bore little relationship to the 'recommendation' being the 'optimum' course of action for the client. Reasons included factors such as which provider paid the highest commission, or hosted the most golf days etc. The plans were also usually sold in a manner that resulted in clients believing that the advice was 'free' because the adviser would be paid by 'the provider'. Why did clients believe that? Easy – because that is what they were told, if charges were disclosed at all!

Of course, that was always a disingenuous claim. The commissions paid to advisers were inevitably recouped from the client in some way - capital units, significant surrender penalties, hidden or confusing charges. This meant that advisers were happy to deal with clients pre-

RDR that they would not deal with in today's adviser charging world because a) pre-RDR commissions could be more than 'generous', b) advisers could avoid having that discussion with clients about fees that they now must have but which some may still feel uncomfortable having, c) post-RDR, the fees that advisers have decided they need to charge are only appropriate for higher worth clients and d) clients can now see the costs more clearly and many choose not to pay or cannot afford to pay. The difference now is that clients at least have half a chance to decide not to incur the cost whereas previously, not only did they not have that opportunity, but they proceeded in blissful ignorance of the cost of 'free advice' … that is until they had to surrender a plan that they could not afford to sustain and which should not have been sold to them in the first place, when the commission that had been paid to the adviser and the consequent surrender penalties often meant that the client made little, no or a negative return. Research at the time showed that the average life span of regular savings contracts was around 4-5 years at which point even a ten-year plan (popular with many advisers) generally carried a hefty surrender penalty.

Now, it is also true that some clients were sold essential life cover or pension savings that they would never have voluntarily bought without a bit of 'adviser' input. Lots of families doubtless had good reason to be grateful for the maturity or death proceeds of the plans that the man from the Pru or the Coop had sold to the father or mother, faithfully collecting the modest premiums in person each week.

Nonetheless, while it seems that many consumers who would benefit from financial advice cannot afford to access it currently, going back to some sort of commission model where the client still pays the cost but just does not realise it is not the answer.

Is there an advice gap? Yes, to some degree, but perhaps also a semantical gap. Much of what is labelled an advice gap is really, in my view, a sales gap – adviser firms cannot or will not sell their product, namely financial advice, at a price that is affordable or appropriate for a significant number of people.

To be fair to advisers, there are costs involved in providing financial advice as currently defined and regulated. That will always mean that advice simply cannot be, and will never be able to be, delivered economically to a significant proportion of the population.

This was acknowledged as far back as December 2014 in the research paper on vulnerability by ESRO on behalf of the FCA.

"There will always be some consumers whose custom will not be valued and desired by some financial services firms due to their limited means."

That is just the reality of the advice sector's current business model and income expectations, both derived largely from the pre-RDR world of commission. This is examined in more detail in Chapter five.

What is the answer? Well, it is self-evident that, if the current adviser business model cannot close the gap, another business model has to step up. In light of the 100% failed attempts to make 'robo-advice' work over the past decade and, despite the currently hyped hopes for artificial intelligence as the solution, it seems staggeringly unlikely that some fundamentally new market disrupting low-cost **advice delivery** model will appear out of left field. So, if **advice** cannot be delivered economically for many consumers, thoughts need to turn to whether differently regulated **guidance** can.

The past decade has seen several attempts to amend the advice/guidance boundary. These were all doomed to failure because making any changes to the regulatory environment around the advice perimeter is not trivial and would require legislation. Another attempt is being made at time of writing (late 2024) and may just have a better chance of success. However, this attempt has very limited ambitions and, importantly, does not see adviser firms as having a part to play.

In its December 2024 Consultation Paper *(CP24/27: Advice Guidance Boundary Review – proposed targeted support reforms for pensions)*, the FCA's proposed 'targeted support' is firmly aimed only at pensions and is clearly not intended to enable financial advisers to play any part – a recognition perhaps of the gap between what advisers keep proclaiming they need to charge and what is an appropriate cost for many consumers – i.e. the sales gap.

The paper states ...

> *"... firms providing targeted support would have to comply with our proposed conduct standards ... We expect advice firms may find it practically difficult to provide targeted support while complying with some of these requirements."*

While the paper explicitly raises concerns that consumers might confuse targeted support with holistic advice, the 'practically difficult' would appear to be as much an acceptance of the reality that targeted support will only be worthwhile if it is able to be delivered on a consumer segment/mass market basis at a substantially lower cost than currently applies generally to financial advice.

Will if this initiative close the sales/advice gap? Time will tell.

Fit for purpose

As will be referred to more than once in later chapters, there has long been an obligation on firms to assess the merits of any tools they use in the suitability process. As far back as March 2011, in its Finalised Guidance on assessing suitability (FG11/15) the regulator stated ...

> *Firms should use a tool only where they are satisfied that it provides outputs that are appropriate and fit for purpose. Firms need to recognise where a tool has limitations and mitigate these in the suitability assessment process.*

This was subsequently formalised in COBS 9A.2.9, which stated that firms should take reasonable steps to ensure:

> *… all tools, such as risk assessment profiling tools or tools to assess a client's knowledge and experience, employed in the suitability assessment process are fit-for-purpose and are appropriately designed for use with their clients, with any limitations identified and actively mitigated through the suitability assessment process …*

The 2011 paper findings suggested that many firms did not understand how the tools they used actually worked, including what they were (and were not) designed to do. Worse, the paper highlighted concerns that out of eleven risk-profiling tools the regulator had reviewed nine had weaknesses which could, in certain circumstances, lead to flawed outputs.

These weaknesses included …

- questions that were not clearly worded, or where the content was unlikely to be understood, and which could result in customers not giving answers that accurately reflect the risk they were willing and able to take
- the increased possibility of customers misunderstanding the questions asked where the

questions were vague, used double negatives or complex language that the customer may not have understood

The paper concluded that poor outcomes could occur if firms ...

- use tools which are not fit for purpose
- do not understand how a tool works or its limitations; or
- fail to mitigate a tool's limitations within the suitability assessment.

Although the identities of the nine offending risk profiling tools were never revealed, it was not difficult to spot the popular third-party tools that were flawed.

The sad reality is that many of these are still popular – and still flawed!

Let's consider just one question format that was around in 2011 and still appears in tools in use today.

The question appears in a number of flavours but all are along the lines of the following examples ...

- *Compared to the average person, I would say I take more risks.*
- *How do you think that a friend who knows you well would describe your attitude to taking financial risks?*
- *Others would say that I like taking risks with my money.*

All these questions share a fatal flaw – namely that they are impossible to answer!

The first requires the client to have knowledge of an 'average person' that nobody possesses. So any response must be a VERY subjective guess at what the client thinks the view of the mythical aforementioned average person might be.

The second and third are even worse as they require clients to read the mind of how another person might read their own mind! It really is all very silly.

Many tools include a number of questions in a similar vein and it is difficult to see how any meaningful appropriate weighted link can be made to a client's attitude to investment risk from the response.

The relevant question here is how many firms/advisers truly understand the way the tools they use work, and the weaknesses that may exist, based on having undertaken an objective assessment that did not merely rely on …

- marketing claims from the tool provider
- lots of firms use it so it must be ok
- it is from <name of 'big' third-party> so it must be ok
- it's psychometric so it must be ok (although we're not quite sure what psychometric actually means)

COBS 9A defines three elements of assessing a client's risk profile – risk tolerance, knowledge and experience and capacity for loss.

Third-party tools all attempt to address the client's risk tolerance but many do not address the client's knowledge and experience. And capacity for loss is not handled well by **any** of the major third-party tools – some do not address it at all.

Similar critique can be applied to Cash Flow Modelling tools used by many firms. In my experience, it is often the case that firms do not appear to have undertaken any due diligence on the tool in an effort to fully understand how and when it should be used or how the tool works under the surface. This is explored in more detail in Chapter three.

It is somewhat ironic then that one of the most effective means of assessing capacity for loss is by preparation of an appropriate cash flow model! In the twilight zone everything is connected.

Finally, there continue to be regular articles in online trade press urging firms to make more/better use of technology or suffer dire consequences. That these articles are almost always authored by a tech business with 'must have' financial services related apps to sell does not escape notice. Many firms will no doubt suffer from FOMO or be attracted to the notion of technology making life easier and profits healthier but care is needed.

The latest 'must have' is of course artificial intelligence (AI). Great excitement and even greater claims surround AI and how it will transform the world. Some adviser firms are already proudly announcing that they are using this or that AI app to good effect. An early candidate for adoption is AI which creates summarised notes of recorded client meetings/calls. Such an app has obvious attractions in terms of reduced admin time. But firms would be well advised to test the accuracy of the output. And to do so themselves rather than merely rely on assurances from app provider. Already, the need for AI disclaimers around online AI generated content has been identified. An example might look like this ...

This website may contain content created by AI or other automated technologies. Such content should not be relied upon for any specific purpose without verification of its accuracy or completeness.

If the accuracy or completeness of such content should not be relied on in the context of a website, I would suggest that blind reliance on it in a client file might be unwise

CHAPTER 2 – ISSUE NUMBER FOUR ... VAT

CHAPTER 2 – ISSUE NUMBER FOUR ...

... VAT

Note that this chapter is based on current law and practice at time of writing (Q4 2024). As with any tax, there may be future changes to rates and thresholds or how the tax is applied. The content provided here is for information only and intended to form a basis for understanding the issues that I believe many firms should be considering.

With the introduction of adviser charging at the end of 2012, many adviser firms were unsure as to whether their services were subject to VAT. Recognising this, HMRC reissued guidance on determining how VAT applies in financial advice firms. This chapter takes account of the HMRC guidance and sets out the main VAT considerations. I suspect many firms may still be unsure or may have let VAT slip out of view as an aspect that needs to be constantly considered. Note that the HMRC guidance relates only to retail investment products as defined by the RDR.

When does VAT apply?

VAT treatment depends upon the service the adviser is providing – the method of payment is not relevant. Generally, the supply of goods and services in the UK is liable to the current standard VAT rate of 20%.

However, in certain cases, a specific exemption is applicable. For IFAs and other financial services suppliers, exemption is available when the service is 'intermediation' - this is defined as 'the bringing together of two parties - a client requiring a financial product and a suitable provider of that product'.

Intermediation and advice cycle steps

Contracting with a client for steps **1 to 5** in figure one would result in the entire service being considered as VAT exempt intermediation. Note that 'Acting between' (step 5) must have the elements normally linked to setting up a financial product - arranging required paperwork and payment for the product. Without step 5 there is no intermediation.

If the original contract for supply changes for any reason, then it should be considered that a new contract has commenced at that point and VAT treatment on the new supply will be determined by the nature of that service in the normal way.

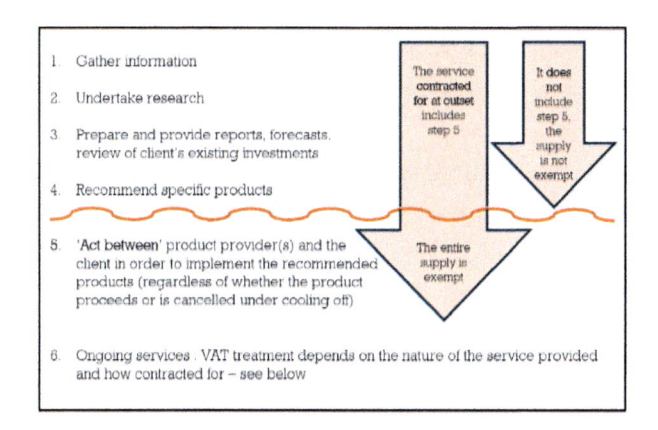

```
1. Gather information                           The service        It does
                                                contracted         not
2. Undertake research                           for at outset      include
                                                includes           step 5,
3. Prepare and provide reports, forecasts,      step 5             the
   review of client's existing investments                         supply
                                                                   is not
4. Recommend specific products                                     exempt
~~~~~~~~~~~~~~~~~~~~~~~~~~~~~~~~~~~~~~~~~~~~~~~~~~~~~~~~~~~~~~~~~~
5. 'Act between' product provider(s) and the    The entire
   client in order to implement the recommended supply is
   products (regardless of whether the product  exempt
   proceeds or is cancelled under cooling off)

6. Ongoing services : VAT treatment depends on the nature of the service provided
   and how contracted for – see below
```

Figure one

Some examples ...

1. A contract for a financial health check that only requires stages 1-3 ... **VAT applies**

2. A contract to recommend specific products that does not include explicit agreement to implement those products ... **VAT applies**. If the client subsequently instructs the adviser to implement the products then this would have to be done under a new contract, which would be ... **VAT exempt**. This exemption would not however apply retrospectively to the original supply.

3. A contract to recommend specific products, including agreement that the client could instruct the adviser to implement some or all of the products as per stage 5. However, the intended transaction does not proceed. The supply is **VAT exempt,** provided the adviser can evidence that intermediary services with a view to arranging a relevant financial product were contracted for and supplied, despite the actual transaction being aborted.

4. As per example 3 but the transaction(s) are in fact implemented ... **VAT exempt.**

Intermediation, separate supplies and predominance

Intermediation will often involve an advice phase, alongside fact finding and research but it is important to note that not all advice will satisfy the conditions to be part of a supply of intermediation. Figure two should help to clarify the different VAT treatments that can arise.

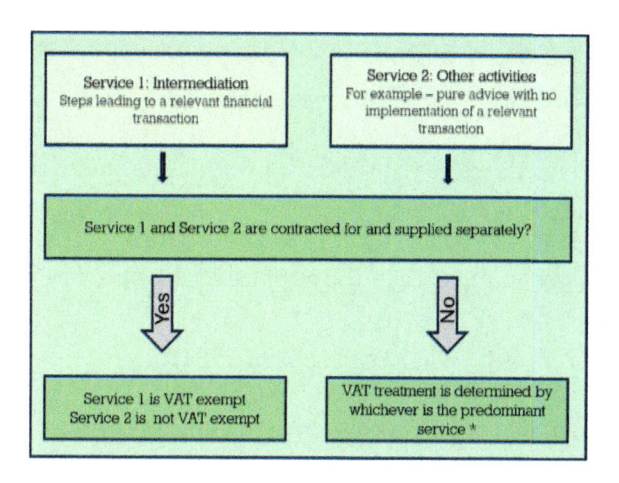

```
┌─────────────────────────────┐  ┌─────────────────────────────┐
│   Service 1: Intermediation │  │ Service 2: Other activities │
│ Steps leading to a relevant │  │ For example - pure advice   │
│   financial transaction     │  │ with no implementation of a │
│                             │  │    relevant transaction     │
└──────────────┬──────────────┘  └──────────────┬──────────────┘
               ↓                                 ↓
┌─────────────────────────────────────────────────────────────┐
│ Service 1 and Service 2 are contracted for and supplied     │
│                       separately?                           │
└──────────────┬──────────────────────────────┬───────────────┘
             Yes ↓                          No ↓
┌─────────────────────────────┐  ┌─────────────────────────────┐
│    Service 1 is VAT exempt  │  │  VAT treatment is determined│
│  Service 2 is not VAT exempt│  │ by whichever is the         │
│                             │  │     predominant service *   │
└─────────────────────────────┘  └─────────────────────────────┘
```

Figure two

* If the predominant element is exempt, the entire supply is exempt. If the predominant element is taxable, the whole supply is taxable. Assessing which element is predominant can be tricky and uncertain. In its guidance, HMRC indicates that adviser services related to 'retail investment products' will normally be regarded as a single supply of VAT exempt services - provided that the client has entered into a **single** contract for a package of services **that includes agreement for the adviser to proceed to arrange the recommended financial products**. But firms' contracts are not always clear in the way they describe the service to be supplied – see later comments regarding evidence.

45

When do firms have to register for VAT?

A firm needs to be registered for VAT if its standard rated turnover ...

- has been more than the applicable threshold in the past twelve months
(threshold = £90,000 as at April 2024)

- is anticipated to go over the current threshold in the following thirty days

Firms can deduct input VAT from related purchases provided the firm is already VAT registered and only supplies taxable services (standard or zero rated). If the firm provides a mixture of taxable and exempt services, it will usually only be able to deduct a proportion of input tax.

The Flat Rate Scheme

Firms with a VAT taxable turnover below £150,000 p.a. (excluding VAT) should consider using the Flat Rate Scheme.

No deduction against input tax is available under the scheme as an allowance has already been included in the rate - 13.5% is the current rate for Financial Services firms.

However, the costs of accounting for VAT will be lower for firms using the scheme.

Stage 6 - ongoing services ...

Most advisers provide ongoing monitoring and review of a client's portfolio. Pre-RDR, this would not generally have been done under any formal contract. In that event, or where the 'contract' was less than specific about the nature of the service to be provided, firms are unlikely to have the evidence that could form one layer of defence against any future HMRC VAT challenge.

> *"Where the customer is seeking the arrangement of a Retail Investment Product and the adviser performs the arrangements as outlined at stage 5 above, (regardless of whether the sale of the product is finally concluded):* **and is able to evidence that they have done so***; the services in stage 1-6, which fall within the agreement concluded with the customer, will be VAT exempt."*
> *VATFIN7665*

The evidence is key. Accordingly, it is highly recommended that every service provided to clients is supported by the evidence of a clear and detailed formal contract of supply.

"Without prejudice to the general VAT evidential requirements, **an adviser will need to keep sufficient evidence to support the tax treatment applied to the services supplied.** *This evidence will need to be specific to the services performed for the customer and demonstrate that the adviser acted between the customer and the product provider with a view to arranging the sale of VAT exempt Retail Investment Products.* **If an adviser is unable to provide evidence that an exempt supply has taken place, VAT will be due on that supply."** *VATFIN7675*

The desirability of a clear contract for supply of the service is not just for the purposes of VAT. It is also good business practice as it enables both the adviser and the client to be clear about what services will be supplied and what will be charged.

The VAT position around ongoing services is likely to be as follows …

- VATFIN7665 indicates that where the ongoing service is provided as part of a **single** contract where the client agrees to stages 1-5 shown in Figure one above, the entire supply from 1-6 is likely to be VAT exempt. The review may be considered as ancillary to the original intermediation.
(Although some might argue that predominance may apply – that the original one-off intermediation service could be considered as the minor partner in the overall

client adviser relationship that is expected to be in place for many years and where the ongoing service does not clearly qualify as intermediation in its own right. HMRC appears to have worded VATFIN7665 on the assumption that all ongoing service provided by advisers qualifies as intermediation – but this is not necessarily the case. And there is the merest hint that HMRC recognised this possibility in VATFIN7670 where it states, "<u>some</u> or all of the process outlined in VATFIN7665 <u>may</u> occur again."

It may be prudent to be aware of the possibility that HMRC might revisit this at some point.

- Where ongoing service is contracted for separately, as a standalone service ... the VAT treatment depends on the nature of the services provided in the normal way. If the service can be shown to satisfy all the conditions of intermediation, then it will be VAT exempt – if not then VAT will apply. See below for further comments around whether ongoing service involves intermediation or not.

Is ongoing service always intermediation?

Whether contracted for as part of the initial advice or as a separate standalone service, HMRC's default assumption underlying VATFIN7665 would appear to have been that an adviser's ongoing service will always meet the definition of VAT exempt intermediation in its own right. That is to say that the ongoing service will include **all** the stages 1 to 5 in Figure one. But that is not necessarily always the case. And HMRC does nod to this possibility by stating that, in ongoing reviews, *"*<u>*some*</u> *or all of the process outlined in VATFIN7665* <u>***may***</u> *occur again"*. The 'may' implies that it is possible that the conditions required for exempt intermediation to exist ***may not*** be present. Let's explore further.

In the early years following RDR, and with ever increasing use of investment platforms, it is likely that advisers envisaged the ongoing reviews they signed most clients up to would generally include the following elements:

- a rebalance the asset allocation within the client's portfolio in order to remain aligned to the client's risk profile
- recommend and implement any changes or new investments

In a perfect world, the contract for supply of the service would reflect this degree of clarity – although it often doesn't. Strictly speaking, the platform is a service not a product but HMRC appears to accept that intermediating products that just happen to be purchased via an investment platform is good enough for exempt intermediation to exist, even where the adviser recommends a model portfolio service on the platform rather than creating a portfolio from a selection of funds chosen by the adviser firm.

But some firms had previously used, and perhaps are still using, fund of funds or multi-manager arrangements as the investment solution. In this case, where is the rebalance? It's done automatically by the provider, not the adviser. The ongoing service ceases to meet the five-stage exempt intermediation conditions?

Apart from VAT considerations, this could also be an important question now because of the changes to Capital Gains Tax (CGT) announced in the October 2024 Budget. The annual allowance has been reduced significantly and CGT rates increased. This could jump start a move away from model portfolios and back to the use of single funds (and arguably should do for some clients).

Discretionary managed portfolios – careful consideration required!

It seems to be the case that many firms have long since moved away from the regular rebalance process that they once so proudly promised. This move was almost certainly largely driven by the non-trivial administrative burden that accompanied each rebalance for any firm that did hold discretionary permissions. In addition to the process of reviewing portfolios and deciding what changes were to be recommended, those changes needed to be set out in a suitability report, provided to the client and the client's formal authority to make the changes obtained. Even where all clients were good as gold and responded quickly in the affirmative, the whole process was a royal PITA!

This resulted in many firms instead using a model portfolio on their preferred platform, but where the portfolio is managed by a discretionary manager (DFM/DIM). At a stroke, all that rebalancing/obtain client authority hassle is removed. Result!

But it raises a couple of questions.

First, if the DFM MPS comprises the entirety of the client's investments, what intermediation is involved in the adviser's annual review service? Second, if the fundamental activity of managing the portfolio is done by the DFM, how does the adviser firm justify the level of ongoing adviser charge? This move to DFM MPS, and the use of platforms, both make life easier for advisers, but it is the client who pays the additional layers of fees involved – and I have not come across any case where there was a reduction in adviser charging to reflect the adviser's lower costs. See Chapter five for a deeper exploration around ongoing reviews.

Leaving the model portfolio scenario to one side for the moment, the basic VAT situation in relation to advisers introducing clients directly to a DFM is that the DFM portfolio is a taxable service, not a product and so the adviser charge to the client for recommending the DFM is subject to VAT. The HMRC VAT manual states:

> *"However, regardless of how it is remunerated, there is no (VAT) exemption for the introduction (by an adviser) of a client to a discretionary investment management service because discretionary investment management is a taxable service that does not fall within the financial services exemptions. The service provided by the IFA is a taxable introduction to a taxable management service. It is not correct for IFAs to look through to the selection and purchase of VAT exempt assets by the discretionary investment manager and treat their services as being exempt introductions to a series of VAT exempt transactions."* HMRC internal manual **VATFIN7600**

So, an adviser's introduction to a DFM where the DFM directly manages the client's portfolio is subject to VAT on the adviser fee charged for the recommendation and introduction. Unfortunately, HMRC guidance is not all encompassing and so it cannot be stated with certainty whether or not this is likely also to be the case where the direct DFM service happens to be available via a platform that is not the DFM's own platform.

The same guidance gaps also create a degree of uncertainty around the use of model portfolios generally. However, the current position appears to be that where advisers recommend and implement investments using model portfolios on a platform, including a DFM managed MPS, that is considered as intermediation of a non-VATable platform service and the adviser fees will not be subject to VAT. Until further notice perhaps! Again, it may be prudent to be aware of the possibility that HMRC might revisit this at some point.

Points to note

- **Separate supplies**
  If you contract with your client for distinct and separate services, each service must be considered separately and VAT applied as appropriate

- **Method of payment**
  The nature of the services contracted and provided for is what determines whether they are exempt or standard rated. The method of payment is irrelevant.

- **Network members**
  Assuming a traditional network model, any services provided to a client are deemed to be provided by the network and not the member for the purposes of VAT. It is the network that should charge the client and apply VAT as required. The member firm is deemed to be providing services to the network and VAT registered members will need to apply VAT (where applicable and if the member is VAT registered) to the charge made to the network. That is the remuneration received from the

network for any non-intermediation services provided to the client on behalf of the network.

- **Evidence**
In the event of a challenge form HMRC, firms need to be able to justify any services provided as exempt.
Suitable evidence would include ...
  - clearly worded marketing material describing the services the client is receiving
  - clear contracts for the supply of the service.

- **Systems and processes**
It is essential that firms have adequate accounting processes in place - firstly to know when registration is required and then to be able to charge and account for VAT as required after registration.

- **... a final thought ...**
As mentioned already, the VAT information here is intended as an overview of how VAT applies in relation to financial advice services. VAT is a complicated tax – hence the copious use here of qualifications such as 'likely' and 'should'. **There is no substitute for taking proper advice from your tax advisers.**

Action

- Firms should discuss the VAT situation with their tax adviser

- Firms should review existing contracts to ensure they are adequate to describe the nature of the service

- Firms should have a process which formally allocates each chargeable interaction with clients as being exempt or non-exempt and ensure that it can support the exempt conclusions with appropriate evidence.

- Firms should monitor this 'log' in order to confirm whether and when VAT registration is required

CHAPTER 3 – ISSUE NUMBER THREE ... PENSION TRANSFERS

CHAPTER 3 – ISSUE NUMBER THREE ...

... PENSION TRANSFERS

Insurance is sold not bought

There is an ages old adage that 'insurance is sold not bought'. Not unreservedly true these days of course. Some, for example motor insurance, is mandatory – although there are still lots of uninsured drivers around. Most other common types of cover, while not mandatory, are widely bought by consumers, albeit often grudgingly, more in fear of the possible difficulties that might arise otherwise than by any great desire to spend money on something that they cannot see or touch and which may never happen. Or in the case of life cover, will inevitably happen but just not yet! Shades of St Augustine to whom is attributed the prayer *"Lord, make me chaste and celibate - but not yet!"*

This situation was arguably also valid in relation to investments up to around 60-70 years ago when stock market investment in any form tended to be a regular pastime only for the wealthier members of UK society. Although a relatively small number of investment trusts and unit trusts had been around for many years, it was arguably not until the 1960s/70s that stock market linked investment started to take off among other UK demographics.

According to The Investment Association, there are currently around 4,700 collective investment funds of varying flavours available to UK investors. Yet, despite this vast choice, and the best efforts of platform operators, fund managers/providers and financial advisers, a significant proportion of the population still apparently chooses to invest in cash rather than equity-based assets.

The FCA's Financial Lives 2022 survey indicated that individuals with between £10k and £20k of investible assets held a whopping 79% of their capital all or mostly in cash. Even those with between £50k and £100k of investible assets held a clear majority of their capital, namely 61%, in cash or mostly in cash. I interpret this as support for my conclusion that there remains a large number of potential yet reluctant UK investors who would require a fair bit of convincing before they would consider moving away from cash into equity based OEICs, ISAs and the like. There are probably as many reasons for this as there are people. In general, it might reasonably be recognised that equity investment is simply not for everyone, driven by perceptions, or misperceptions, of investment risk. This is fair enough and I firmly believe that it is entirely inappropriate for the FCA or advisers to play 'Nanny knows best' or wag a proverbial finger at people for 'missing out' because they don't avail themselves of financial advice and the 'growth potential' of stock market linked investments.

The FCA has stated that one of its desired outcomes is a *'20% reduction in the number of consumers with higher risk tolerance holding over £10k in cash by 2025'.*

In my view and leaving aside for a moment questions around how cash holding consumers' risk tolerance would be identified, and the possibility that these consumers sticking with cash may be a pretty good indicator of a lower risk tolerance, this desired outcome is simply an arbitrary and inappropriate 'target' for the regulator to aim at. It is perfectly valid for people to be risk averse by choice or nature or to hold any amount or proportion of their investible assets in cash for other reasons, regardless of their risk tolerance or level of financial acumen. Whatever the reason so many people stick to cash, there would appear to be a large element of *'investments are sold not bought'* running alongside the old insurance version.

And that probably reflects, with a high degree of accuracy, the career experience of many advisers when they meet with potential new clients who do not fall into the high net worth or otherwise financially savvy category. These rather more middle of the road clients, that are arguably the meat and drink of many firms' target market, do not generally throw money at financial advisers, with a pressing desire for it to be invested in capital at risk instruments. Instead, they may tend to have a need to be persuaded of the medium to long term benefits of investing other than in cash. And if they do invest, many may need regular reassurance when their investments take an inevitable dip. I recognise that there are broad generalisations here, and also reference to a survey whose results may or may not be seamlessly transferrable to the population as a whole. However, as this entire book is based on personal observations from my fifty plus years of experience in financial services, and awareness of the views of many colleagues, advisers and clients over the period, I have to say that I believe my observations are close to the mark.

Advisers' general experience over so many years of having to persuade (~~one might say sell~~) reluctant clients to insure or invest, selling the benefits of a recommended solution and working to a fee model whereby the adviser only gets paid when (~~a product is sold~~) the client accepts the adviser's recommendation to insure or invest is simply the reality of the UK financial advice world over the past few decades.

Unfortunately, I think this accumulated adviser mindset that clients need to be persuaded to invest may have resulted in a number of unintended and unfortunate consequences. Old habits die hard and, when presented with the 'business opportunity' of George Osborne's pension freedoms in 2015, many advisers seem not to have recognised that the 'transfer client' was a fundamentally new type of beast!

We will come back to that later.

We've been here before

I was around when the original pension transfer mis-selling scandal arose in the 1980s/90s. By then I had moved on from advising, managing teams of advisers and a variety of senior roles within a national adviser firm, Instead, I had left the safety of an employed position behind, set up a consultancy business and was providing consultancy services to firms, working mostly with some well-known banks and providers.

At the height of the pensions mis-selling scandal, I landed a major project to help one large regional firm redo their review and redress project. The firm's first attempt had been found by the regulator to be seriously flawed and had failed to identify a large number of clients who had been recommended to transfer out of a defined pension scheme when that was not in the client's best interests.

That industry wide pensions review involved in the region of 1.6 million consumers. Quite apart from the obvious impact for around half a million of those consumers who were subsequently assessed as having suffered financial detriment, the debacle had serious consequences for the industry - (providers were involved too – many had a tied sales force). When the dust finally settled, the FSA indicated that the scandal had cost insurers and financial advisers at least £11.8bn in compensation payments – with the significant additional costs of implementing the review also being incurred. The FSA also took disciplinary action against 346 firms, resulting in fines totalling just under £10m.

So it was with a mixture of déjà vu and not a little disappointment in our financial services industry that I saw a whole new, possibly bigger*, pension transfer scandal had reared its head barely a couple of decades later, as a result of what many believed was the rather hasty introduction of pensions freedoms in April 2015.

(* Past business review/redress continues in some firms at time of writing so and it is difficult to pin down any reliable data around number of transfers made since April 2015 or how many will have resulted in redress or the amount of redress and other costs involved. It is fair to assume that the average transfer values will probably far exceed those that applied in the original pensions review. It is of note that the redress bill for British Steel [BSPS] related transfers alone was well north of £100m by mid-2023. Over the period in question, a significant number of non BSPS transfers have also been subject to FCA instructed past business reviews or Section 166 reports, with consequent redress. Total amount of redress might well be understated as many cases have ended up being compensated by the FSCS or via FOS where compensation award limits restrict the true amount of redress that should have been paid.. Firms would also have had substantial costs on top of the redress in undertaking past business reviews or Section 166 reports.)

Were pensions set free too hastily?

Did the 2015 changes cause the subsequent consumer detriment arising from unsuitable transfer advice?

Even at the time, many commentators were concerned that the relevant legislation, the Pension Schemes Act 2015, was implemented too quickly, having only been announced in the March 2014 Spring Budget. That view has been repeated in subsequent years by many commentators with the added benefit of hindsight and the added political pressure stemming from Members of Parliament involving themselves, rightly on behalf of their constituents, but not always with adequate understanding, in the British Steel pension scheme debacle. All of which generally ended with accusations from various MPs and others, and 'findings' from several worthy parliamentary committees that the FCA had been inadequately prepared for the impact of the new legislation. I think it is fair to conclude that the FCA were indeed not fully ready to supervise this new situation. It is also fair to suggest that the FCA was dropped in the proverbial by the Government's rapid introduction of pensions freedoms and dropped in it again by the Government's handling of the BSPS situation. Needless to say there was little to no criticism of the Government's part in all of this, despite the obvious background to the BSPS problems being a desire to assist TATA Steel UK Limited (TSUK), the sponsoring employer for the British Steel scheme (BSPS), or more specifically to protect the British jobs involved.

It's not necessary here to describe in detail the changes that TSUK made to the BSPS. That detail is freely available online for anyone sufficiently interested to find it. All that matters for immediate purposes is to note that the Department for Work and Pensions (DWP) was involved in consultations with TSUK around options for restructuring the BSPS as part of an overall plan to stem TSUK's business losses. The DWP concluded that agreement to separate BSPS from TSUK through a Regulated Apportionment Arrangement (RAA) whereby the Pension Protection Fund (PPF) would be involved was a good outcome. As a result, the BSPS pension scheme duly entered the PPF.

BSPS members were given a choice to stay with the BSPS, effectively the PPF, or move into a new BSPS 2 scheme. This exercise was called *Time to Choose*.

Even a most cursory look at the numbers of members involved, the clearly inadequate admin resources within TSUK to deal with the likely number of member enquiries about transferring and the time frame within which members had to 'choose' suggests that the exercise might better have been labelled *'Not enough time to choose'*.

Regulatory oversight of BSPS came under the Pensions Regulator.

The FCA had no jurisdiction in the scheme changes and consequently had played no part.

Another report, critical of the FCA, was published in November 2024. See comments in the shaded box in the following pages.

November 2024 APPG report criticising the FCA

It is of interest, at least to me, that, regardless of my view of what should have been more widely shared blame described above, the BSPS situation was included in yet another parliamentary report, highly critical of the FCA. This 358-page report was published by the grandly titled ' All-Party Parliamentary Group on investment fraud and fairer financial services' (APPGonifandffs).

Here is how the UK Parliament website describes APPGs.

"All-Party Parliamentary Groups (APPGs) are informal cross-party groups that have no official status within Parliament. They are run by and for Members of the Commons and Lords, though many choose to involve individuals and organisations from outside Parliament in their administration and activities."

The report references a number of previous reports, such as this extract from the Work and Pensions Committee 2021 report on how best to tackle the increase in investment frauds following the introduction of 'pension freedoms' in 2015.

"It raised concerns about not only the FCA's operational effectiveness but also the integrity of the evidence it gave the inquiry:

'The FCA told us that there have been a very large number of prosecutions involving scams and unauthorised business. We do not agree with this assessment. Its own figures - revealed only through Freedom of Information requests - show that there were just 25 convictions."

Ignoring the inappropriate conflation of prosecutions and convictions, and the scope for different interpretations of 'very large number', it should be noted that prosecutions are only one mechanism by which the FCA goes about its business. The FCA Handbook states "The FCA's general policy is to pursue through the criminal justice system all those cases where criminal prosecution is appropriate." But they can also refer the case to another prosecuting authority. And putting a prosecution together is not a trivial or inexpensive matter. Investigation and gathering of evidence can take months and years and then there can be a significant delay in court time being allocated. There is a huge amount of supervision and enforcement work done that does not involve a prosecution. This work is the everyday task and relates to individuals and firms that are actually authorised by the FCA. By way of contrast, in its response to a freedom of information request (ref: FOI9358) the FCA pointed out that the majority of the individuals convicted in the period covered by the FOI request were not actually authorised by the FCA.

And, in a seemingly circular recycling of one not entirely fair report to support another, the APPG November 2024 report also references and summarises the BSPS report as follows:

"The National Audit Office's ('NAO') Investigation into the British Steel Pension Scheme . This evaluated the regulatory response to the provision of advice by independent financial advisers that resulted in some 8000 members of the British Steel Pension Scheme (a 'gold-plated' defined benefit one) transferring savings out of it and into personal, defined contribution arrangements. Much (perhaps most) of that advice was flawed, with financial incentives influencing its quality. The NAO is careful to avoid overt criticism of the FCA, though its findings of fact are concerning."

Now, as is recognised in this book, it is undoubtedly the case that 'much, perhaps most' of the financial advice provided to BSPS members was flawed. But to describe the BSPS as 'gold plated' is disingenuous in the extreme. The phrase is ultimately meaningless but deliberately emotive, intended to suggest the best of the best. In fact, the gold plating was already extremely thin, if there was any at all! As described above, the scheme was going to be closed one way or the other, leaving members only with essentially poorer options available (including the poor in many 'perhaps most' cases option of transferring out), the two 'scheme options' arising with Government involvement. The two scheme options were described on the BSPS website.

"BSPS members now have two options: to switch to a new scheme (the New BSPS) providing the same benefits as BSPS but with

lower future increases, or to remain with the current BSPS and move into the Pension Protection Fund (PPF)."

It is also noted that the report includes many 'comments of support' about the report. For example:

"From the Most Reverend and Right Honourable Justin Welby, Archbishop of Canterbury and New City Agenda Advisory Board Member, who said: 'New City Agenda's report into cultural change in the UK's financial regulators is an important piece of work which reminds us that restoring trust requires regulators to practise what they preach.'"

It seems to me that any such report should stand or fall on its content and should not need 'supporting comments'.

Needless to say, the FCA has sought to defend itself from the gist of the report's findings. Chief Executive Nikhil Rathi has stated that the FCA was not given an opportunity to respond to testimonies or findings in advance, nor was it provided with a copy of the report before publication. He also said that the FCA does not feel the picture painted by the APPG report is one it experiences day-to-day, and that "We will always stay focused on improving our operational performance, but I don't think it would be fair to characterise the position as nothing has happened." Another senior spokesperson also disagreed with the characterisation of the MP's statement saying that he did not feel it to be a "fair representation of what is a very difficult job".

I am not suggesting that the FCA is perfect. Nor am I suggesting that the APPG report is entirely without merit or that the individuals involved as APPG members or those who provided input are without some degree of credibility. It is just that the report seems to be that familiar after the event hindsight carping from the sidelines while not fully recognising that at least some of the 'issues' with public organisations that are the subject of the inquiry or committee report may actually be the result of resourcing or legislative shortfalls that can ultimately be traced back to decisions made by consecutive governments.

I don't think that anyone, including the FCA, would claim that the FCA is perfect. Of course there have been issues with firms, despite the existence of regulators and regulations. Some rule changes have been slower to appear than would have been ideal, for example the banning of contingent charging for transfer advice to address identified problems with pension transfer advice. It is surely in the nature of any regulatory beast that regulations intended to result in good practice can be set *proactively*. Just as surely, given human nature, it is inevitable that some of the human beings to whom those regulations apply will adopt poor practices, contrary to the requirements, to which the regulator can only be *reactive*.

In my view, like many a public organisation, the FCA has arguably been expected to do too much with too little.

The FCA started life with three primary objectives:

- protect consumers – securing an appropriate degree of protection for consumers
- protect financial markets – protecting and enhancing the integrity of the UK financial system
- promote competition – we promote effective competition in the interests of consumers

Since August 2023, Parliament added a 'secondary objective' (whatever secondary means in this context – surely an objective is an objective), namely *facilitating the international competitiveness of the UK economy and its growth in the medium to long term'*, which is clearly a complex objective involving many intertwined yet unpredictable geopolitical and market events over which the FCA has little, or at best very limited, influence.

According to the 23/24 accounts, the FCA regulates the conduct of nearly 42,000 firms, and that is after they had cancelled the permissions of 1,261 firms, double the cancellations in the previous year. And those 42,000 firms cover a broad range of activities and types, from advisers to providers to fund managers and platform operators to claims management and credit related firms. Not an easy portfolio!

The FCA had to work through all the rule changes required to reflect the UK's withdrawal from the EU – no trivial task.

Additional responsibilities were added during the period, for example the regulation of Claims Management Companies in April 2019.

None of the above are excuses, just facts.

So, the FCA is undoubtedly not perfect. But to expect that the FCA can pre-empt and prevent absolutely everything that goes wrong in UK financial services is unrealistic. It is akin to expecting that the police can prevent all crimes from being perpetrated – and then blaming the police for the transgressions of the perpetrators!

As if responding to recent criticism and ever-increasing expectations, in a December 2024 letter to the Chancellor Rachel Reeves, the FCA reflected this position, stating,

"The reality is we will never operate a zero-failure regulatory regime. That would stifle innovation at a cost not just to business but consumers too. We will always have to make judgements about how best to deploy our resources. It is not feasible to pursue every piece of intelligence or concern raised about the 42,000 firms we regulate nor all complaints we receive on unauthorised activity."

That seems to me to be a fair and honest appraisal of the real world that the FCA inhabits. So, a bit less counsel of perfection from critics with an agenda and a bit more recognition of the real-world constraints that any large organisation works under in an ever more resource scarce and complicated world might not be a bad idea.

However, while the FCA may be less at fault around the BSPS debacle than it is accused of, it has to be acknowledged that the FCA was and remains responsible for regulating pension transfer advice. And a key part of the pension freedoms legislation is that any individual wishing to transfer safeguarded benefits out of a defined benefit (DB) pension scheme such as BSPS is required to take financial advice from a qualified pension transfer specialist where the proposed transfer involves a DB pension or other safeguarded benefits worth more than £30,000. According to the FCA, this mandatory requirement imposed by the Pensions Schemes Act 2015 was *"to ensure members of DB schemes fully understood the benefits they may be giving up if they transferred to a DC scheme, as well as the risks involved, and could make an informed decision"*. All very laudable - at first sight – yet it created several unfortunate and unintended consequences, not least for scheme members wishing to transfer, which I will not go into here.

Where did this mandatory advice requirement take us? Well, pension freedoms created an obvious and substantial revenue bonanza for financial advisers. Suddenly, out of the blue, advisers could easily identify and access a potentially enormous cohort of people with pretty sizable amounts of money available to invest and who **had** to take advice! Talk about low hanging fruit! Anyone with a passing awareness of previous financial services mis-selling scandals could see this was unlikely to end well!

It was all George's fault

Some commentators have laid the blame for pension transfer mis-selling since 2015 on the Chancellor who created the environment which enabled it with the Pension Schemes Act 2015. Namely one George Osborne. That can certainly be argued but should be considered in the context of why the freedoms were felt to be required in the first place. And it is worth noting that the Act was published under the 2010 to 2015 Conservative and Liberal Democrat coalition government. The Minister of State for Pensions at the time was the Liberal Democrat, Steve Webb.

A key piece of the background to pension freedoms was the continuing decline of annuity rates. Prior to the 2015 Act, people who had saved for many years in a defined contribution pension were obliged to buy an annuity when they wanted to commence taking income from their pension plan(s). But annuity rates had been declining for years and had reached a long time low by the 2010s. Although there were readily identifiable reasons for decreasing rates – primarily reduced interest rates and improved mortality – there was undoubtedly an unfairness arising from the mandatory constraint of having to buy an annuity with the pension fund.

The problem was further exacerbated by the fact that many simply converted the capital to an annuity with whichever provider their pension plan was with and so lost out on a higher annuity rate that may well have been available on the open market. The difference could be significant - as much as around 20%. Perhaps even more if the client had health issues and might have been eligible for enhanced rates.

The table below shows examples of the immediate annuity that could be purchased with a pension fund of £100k.

Year	Annuity
1990	£8,250
1995	£7,250
2000	£7,000
2005	£5,250
2010	£5,250
2015	£4,000

So someone who had accumulated £100k and retired in 2010 would have received an income throughout life some 31.25% higher than another individual with the same accumulated fund who just happened to retire five years later. In fact, there was some evidence at the time that some self-employed people were choosing to delay retirement in what would turn out to be a forlorn hope that annuity rates might improve when, in practice, the rates continued to worsen.

One way or another, there was a degree of pressure on the Government to address the issue and the Pension Schemes Act 2015 was the result. That almost inevitable unintended consequences ensued is irrefutable. But it must be conceded that they meant well!

Thus, the government of the day can be allocated a share of the 'blame' for creating the environment in which large numbers of unsuitable pension transfers would take place. But the very obvious and inescapable fact is that every one of those unsuitable transfers could only be done with the involvement and recommendation of a financial adviser, indeed a pension transfer **specialist** (although we will expand on the latter shortly).

Unregulated Introducers

What about the activities of the many unregulated introducers that seemed to pop up after RDR. Did they contribute to the pension transfer mis-selling that occurred? The timing is no coincidence. RDR required all advisers who wished to continue to advise, to achieve at least a Level 4 qualification. Anecdotal evidence strongly suggests that many of the unregulated introducing firms were founded and peopled by former advisers who, for one reason or another, had decided not to bother attaining the relevant qualification. Certainly that appeared to be the background of the many unregulated introducers I came across since 2015.

Leading up to and certainly following the pension freedoms coming into play, many of these firms/individuals seem to have quickly locked on to the brilliant wheeze of finding 'alternative assets' that could be acceptable within a SIPP and which would pay a handsome commission to any firm directing investment into that asset. Ah yes, commission - just like the good old days before RDR came along and ruined everything!

The list of 'alternative assets' is depressingly long and will be familiar to many readers. It included the usual suspects … holiday or hotel developments in far flung places, Brazilian teak forests, car park space ownership. And some of these alternative assets even actually existed – for a while! The most common features of the various assets were the aforementioned hefty commission payable to the introducer, effectively reducing the client's investment value from day one, and the fact that most of the developments seem to have been doomed to failure from outset and/or run by less than honourable individuals.

The response from unregulated introducers to this perfect storm of commission paying assets and pension freedoms was to market 'free pension reviews' to an unsuspecting public. These reviews of course were 'purely for information', as if offered for some selfless charitable reason, and 'did not constitute regulated advice'. All well and good, except for two things:

- the reason the reviews were offered was far from selfless for the introducers who were undoubtedly swayed by the availability of a substantial commission revenue stream if only they could persuade people to make their pension fund available for investment through the 'free pension review' scam
- the way that many of the introducers implemented the 'non-advice' review actually fell foul of the rules by including elements that constituted regulated advice and/or contravening the introducer rules

I won't go into all the intricacies of the introducer rules here – read FCA PERG 8.33 if you want more detail. The key aspect on which unregulated introducers fell down is that their introductions were only excluded from the need to be regulated provided that the person to whom introductions were to be made was:

- *an authorised person ... AND*
- *the introduction was made* **with a view to the provision of independent advice or the independent exercise of discretion in relation to investments generally or in relation to any class of investments to which the arrangements relate.**

This is known to applicable cognoscenti as the Article 29 defence.

The first of these conditions was met by definition. The leads arising from the 'free pension review' activity were passed on to a tame financial adviser firm. They had to be as transfer funds (if over £30k) could only be made available for investment if the scheme trustees received confirmation from a duly authorised adviser that transfer advice had been provided to the member.

The second condition was where it could and did fall down. Each unregulated introducer tended to have links to a favourite one or sometimes a few of the alternative investment 'opportunities'. The advisers to whom a lead was provided just happened to recommend or encourage the client not only to transfer but also to invest at least some of the transfer value in the particular investment(s) that the introducer had links with. Coincidence? Absolutely not. Independent advice? Absolutely not.

I acted as an expert witness for the FCA in a high-profile case they were prosecuting against one unregulated introducer. My involvement was because a Section 166 report I had created relating to an adviser firm that was involved with unregulated introducers formed a significant element of the FCA's case against the introducer. The relevant part of the S166 report stated:

> *"We found that the firm's advice process did not meet the standards required of independent advice. As has been detailed elsewhere, the reports did not actually state any rationale for the client to invest in the NMI(s)* but merely listed the risks involved. The adviser appears merely to have acquiesced in enabling the NMI* and positioned it firmly as an investment the client wanted prior to having been introduced – the approach being 'here are the risks but since you want it I will arrange it for you'.*
> *The fact that the 'X' investment was only done for clients introduced by 'Y' suggests that the only reason it was used was to meet a formal or informal obligation to the introducer. Otherwise, if it was considered an appropriate investment, we would expect it to have been used for other clients too, if the process behind the investment was truly independent." (* NMI = Non-mainstream pooled investment)*

It seemed clear to me that the adviser had a financial conflict of interest in 'recommending' the introducer's favourite investment, the incentive being to maintain a flow of future leads to be 'advised'.

The Article 29 defence had a third pillar and this also failed at Court. The benefit of the exemption under

Article 29 is lost if the arranging party receives a reward or pecuniary advantage, which is not accounted for to the client. As the introducer received commission in respect of the underlying investments, the judge held that Article 29 could not apply.

So the introducer's activities failed to satisfy the conditions necessary to be exempt from being regulated and that was the basis of the prosecution. The FCA alleged, and the Court found, that the introducer engaged in arranging and promoting investments without FCA authorisation and made false and misleading statements to investors which induced them to transfer their pensions into self-invested personal pensions (SIPPs) and subsequently into alternative investments.

A just and happy ending? Regrettably not.

Although the FCA won its case for a restitution order against the defendants, it later cautioned that this was unlikely to be satisfied. In a letter to investors, the FCA stated that investors were only likely to receive a small fraction of the £11m in compensation which they were owed. The letter stated: *"On present information about the scale of the losses and the value of the assets of the defendants, it is likely that there will be a considerable shortfall."*

So it is undoubtedly the case that unregulated introducers made a major contribution to many scheme members receiving unsuitable pension transfer advice and that significant financial detriment ensued from the introductions.

But again, the very obvious, inescapable and sad fact is that every one of those unsuitable transfers could only be done with the involvement of a financial adviser.

What went wrong?

Know what you need to know

The original pension review process was defined in detail by the regulator and was mandatory. With regard to the firm that I referred to earlier, a primary reason for its failed first attempt at the pension review was a basic lack of knowledge and understanding of the applicable regulatory requirements for transfer advice and how the review process stages were intended to be implemented.

Having been involved in a number of pension transfer related Section 166 reviews of firms since 2015, and having reviewed more pension transfer recommendations than I could shake a stick at, I have to conclude that poor transfer advice was generally caused by a combination of:

- Insufficient knowledge of the regulatory requirements around transfer advice
- Poor objective setting, lack of lateral thinking and inappropriate use of tools
  AND
- Temptation

Let's take a closer look.

Insufficient knowledge

From as early as 2007, there was a requirement for any pension transfer recommendation to be made – or checked - by a 'pension transfer specialist' (PTS). The PTS was defined as *'an individual appointed by a firm to check the suitability of a pension transfer or pension opt-out who has passed the required examinations'*. Fair enough – transfer advice is complex and requires a high level of pension technical knowledge. That knowledge would be gained and evidenced by the individual taking and passing the prescribed exam qualification.

Firms also had the option, and many used it, of allowing any of the firm's non-PTS advisers to provide transfer advice – provided it was 'checked' by a PTS. Again, seems reasonable. The real-life problem was that while the PTS may have gained and been assessed by examination as having sufficient pension technical knowledge, knowledge of the regulatory requirements was often lacking . And any non-PTS adviser could recommend a transfer with effectively little or no technical knowledge and, in my experience, no knowledge at all of the regulatory requirements. This 'accident waiting to happen' situation was exacerbated by PTS 'checking' that was often little more than lip service and a rubber stamp.

Either way, in all the many transfer cases I have reviewed over the years, unsuitable advice was rarely, if ever, a result of some technical knowledge issue. **Overwhelmingly, unsuitable transfer advice was the result of compliance failings.**

Now, I don't think it is unreasonable to expect that financial advisers, who after all work in a regulated environment, should have an adequate grasp of what the regulations have to say about the various activities in which they take part day after day by dint of being a financial adviser. Especially so for those advisers and firms that, in the face of the transfer bonanza from April 2015, actually did 'specialise' in providing only pension transfer advice. Yet, my experience is that many carried on regardless and in blissful ignorance of key regulatory requirements.

The transfer specific rules are contained in the FCA Handbook under COBS 19. As at April 2015, when the pension freedoms bonanza was charging over the horizon, COBS 19 comprised fewer than 1,300 words, all of which had applied since 2007, 2012 or 2013.

The full post-freedoms version of the rules took effect from June 2015 and comprised a mighty word count of just over 1,600.

So what?

Well, the average general adult reading speed in the UK is around 150-250 words per minute. Even using the lower figure, it should have taken around 11 minutes for anyone who needed to have a good awareness of the rules to read. Let's be realistic and allow that the content probably needed to be read a few times to ensure understanding. If it needed ten reads, the time commitment would still have been less than a couple of hours. Not a huge ask given that it is unarguably true that advisers need to know what they need to know in order to do their job properly. In the case of pension transfer advice, the FCA rules are undoubtedly part of that required body of knowledge. Acquiring that knowledge does not appear to have been a major time commitment but it seems to have been a commitment that many firms and advisers didn't bother to make.

Even today, the word count for the April 2024 rules is only around 3,510 words, ignoring the broader rules around abridged advice and contingent charging. Maybe a half hour read? Not much to ask.

Poor objective setting, lack of lateral thinking and inappropriate use of 'tools'

Poor objective setting

The starting point for every piece of financial advice is the fact find. After all, without knowing the client's situation, it is pretty much impossible to comment with any credibility on what he or she should do. It also happens to be contrary with specific FCA rules, in particular COBS 9.2.6, which has been around since 2007:

> *If a firm does not obtain the necessary information to assess suitability, it must not make a personal recommendation to the client or take a decision to trade for him.*

And you would think that identifying the client's needs and objectives would be lesson 101 when advisers are acquiring fact finding skills. Against this background, it has been a continuing mystery to me that so many advisers seem to be unable, or unwilling, to identify meaningful client objectives. Over many years I have come to categorise the 'objectives' that commonly appear in suitability reports as follows:

- **The 'you wanted' objectives**
    These objectives start life in what the adviser intends to recommend. That usually small and pretty standard set of recommendations is then magically transformed backwards into a series of statements suggesting that the client wanted what was going to be recommended. It is usually quite obvious that the client would not ever have made those statements, not least because they appear nowhere in fact finding notes but first come to light in the later suitability report. And some use

terminology that the average client is unlikely to even know. A good example that used to regularly pop up is, 'You wanted a smoothed fund.'. I would suggest that the clients were unlikely to have heard the phrase 'smoothed fund' until the adviser showed up, or worse, until (s)he read it in the suitability report. Oh, and by the way, the recommended product was always from Prudential! Quelle surprise! Excuse my French.

Sometimes there is a reverse 'you wanted', i.e. a statement that the client did not want to do X or Y at this time. For example, 'you do not want to consider life cover at this time', or you do not want to consider your IHT situation at this time'. These reverse wants are often paired with a statement along the lines of, 'you just want to have recommendations for investing £X / switching your plan to a new one'. This always comes across as an indication that the adviser was only focused on the quick and easy wins, so avoiding the need to get involved with the less rewarding, more complex or time consuming client needs. As Shakespeare might have written, *"Whither the oft claimed but oft absent 'holistic advice' or 'financial planning'."*

- **The meaningless objectives**
  There are usually several objectives listed in the

suitability report, after all you can't have too many! So a meaningless one or two often appears alongside one or more of the other types listed here. A typical example would be, 'You wanted to review your pension.' What does that mean? What was the purpose of the review? Merely reviewing it does not achieve any outcome and a true objective should be an outcome – some desired future position. Of course, the not very well-hidden message here is that it is the adviser who wants to 'review' the pension (or other existing plan) which is seen as a source of funds that can be switched or transferred to a new plan. More about this in chapter four.

- **The 'same strokes for different folks' objectives**
  These are simply a standard list of statements that are used in all reports. This can arise where a standard suitability report template is used and never personalised to the particular client's situation. The list would usually include some of the other types mentioned here, for example, the meaningless or leading statements. The problem is that the list is the same for every client leading to formulaic suitability reports that lack credibility.

- **The leading objectives**
  These types may appear to be one of the others.

That is, they may be 'you wanted', or meaningless or bog standard. But what additionally differentiates the leading objective is an insidious and cynical manipulation of the client. The manipulation arises from framing a position in such a way that the answer is at the same time predictable yet meaningless. It is what might be called the 'Mom and apple pie' question. Ask most people if they are in favour of mothers and popular classic desserts and the response is pretty likely to be positive. The problem is, so what? Well, if most people would be likely to respond in a particular way, the response isn't going to add much to the sum of human knowledge – or the efficacy of the fact find.

And so it is with leading objectives, which have featured strongly in so many pension transfer cases I have seen. It is reasonable to suggest that the key features of pension freedoms that came to be in 2015 could be summarised as 'flexibility and control' in the shape of:

- o The option to draw tax free cash from age 55
- o Cash can be drawn without having to take 'pension' at the same time
- o The amount of income can be varied up and down as required

- The fund remaining in the event of death can pass to children/others

With very little amendment, these features of a drawdown plan tended to be the objectives listed in many pension transfer reports, simply prefaced with a 'You would like …'. This practice was so universally present in transfer suitability reports that it is difficult to conclude other than that it was nothing more than the Mom and apple pie scenario applied in order to create reasons to recommend a transfer.

Who would not want the option to draw cash from age 55 while not having to take taxable income until needed later – all with the added bonus of a nice nest egg to leave to the kids? What should have been established was whether the client had any intention of drawing the cash at age 55, i.e. actually using the option. If not, then it is not an objective for this client even if the option is there in the product, and so does not add any support to the suitability of the recommendation to transfer despite being used as justification for a transfer recommendation.

This 'features as objectives' approach was always formulaic and essentially misleading. Especially when they were contrasted unfavourably (and usually unfairly) with the client's final salary scheme – *'under your scheme you would have to early retire to get cash at 55 and would have to take pension at the same time and that pension would suffer an early retirement penalty and cannot not be varied once you start it'*. No mention of final salary guarantees, survivor benefits, lifetime sustainability, no personal charges and no personal investment risk!

This was certainly what I saw in virtually every transfer client file for several years following April 2015. The laziness of using 'flexibility and control' as client objectives was eventually roundly criticised by the FCA but not until several years had passed since 2015 and so many clients had been manipulated by the leading objective habit. In FG21/3, the FCA stated:

> *"The aim of establishing the client's objectives is to understand their priorities, their plans and what motivates them.* **Objectives should not be generic but should be personal to every client. Features of the pension freedoms are not client objectives. If your firm gives advice based on objectives such as 'flexibility' or 'control of my pension', these are unlikely to be sufficiently personalised to**

> *enable you to provide a suitable personal recommendation, without further detail.* You should challenge vague statements like these and identify the underlying reasons why your client needs or wants these features."

Applying this thought process to the generic 'flexibility and control' objectives would either firmly confirm them as genuine objectives of the particular client or exclude them as a basis for recommending a transfer.

For example, of course it's always nice to have options but, as mentioned above, what matters in the advice world is which options are actually relevant, that the client actually needs and being able to evidence that with additional information. So, the suitability report might state that the client wants the option of taking cash at age 55 (although there was rarely any note of this in the fact find or meeting notes). Why? What likely and credible situation does the client envisage that indicates that this option is not merely a 'nice to have' but reasonably likely to be used by the client to address an identified need? Is this documented on the client file?

Similarly, what is the anticipated situation that will be best suited by the ability to vary income withdrawals?

And how realistic were the stated 'desired' objectives anyway? Again, it would be nice to be able to leave the remaining pension fund to the next generation but, in so many cases, it was not realistic, and certainly not guaranteed, that there would be any significant residual fund once the client's lifetime needs were satisfied. So the weight of this desire as a driver for a transfer recommendation was often pretty minimal. You get the point, I could go on – I often do.

Yet so many transfer recommendations were based on the leading 'objectives' of flexibility and control. And, in so many cases, the formulaic story put together on the basis of these factors could not survive close scrutiny. It is therefore entirely unsurprising that so much unsuitable advice was provided and subsequently found to be wanting.

Lack of lateral thinking

I expect most readers will be familiar with the saying, *"If it looks like a duck, walks like a duck and quacks like a duck, then it just may be a duck."*

The philosophical concept known as Occam's Razor suggests that this is a reasonable logic to apply in everyday life. The most obvious and simplest answer is probably the right answer.

However, in my experience, this approach led to many transfer recommendations being unsuitable or at least unsafe.

The problem was that clients would contact advisers for advice about transferring a pension and the adviser would immediately lock the case mentally as transfer advice. This forever narrowed the adviser's thought process and negated any hint of lateral thinking.

We need to briefly revisit objectives here. A robust exploration of the client's objectives might identify that the client actually needed advice that was not limited to 'transfer or not'. Some typical examples:

Client objective as stated in the suitability report

1. Draw cash and repay debt / mortgage
2. Leave a legacy to children
3. To not 'lose' the value of the pension on death before retirement
4. Ability to vary income
5. Transfer now to lock in 'highest ever' transfer values
6. Transfer now, X years in advance of intended retirement

Transfer is one option but these should also be considered …

1. Mortgage advice, refer to debt counselling
2. IHT planning, life cover
3. Life cover – term or whole life as appropriate. Explain scheme survivor benefits
4. Take final salary pension and use other defined contribution pensions or other assets to provide a degree of variable income as required
5. Explain that it is not possible to know that transfer values are at their peak any more than it is possible to time stock market cycles with certainty.

> 6. Explain that the transfer decision does not need to be made immediately and deferring transfer to nearer intended retirement will enable continued benefit of escalation and death in service benefits

This lateral thinking is in fact explicitly covered in COBS 19.1.6 which states that, in order to assess suitability of a transfer, the factors that firms should consider includes, *"alternative ways to achieve the retail client's objectives instead of the transfer".*

Yet consideration of alternative possible non-transfer options just didn't feature in many of the transfer cases I reviewed. The failure to at least consider all potentially valid options was almost always sufficient to assess the advice as unsuitable or at least unsafe and open to future challenge. There is long standing regulatory guidance that firms should only consider a transfer to be suitable if it can clearly demonstrate, on contemporary evidence, that the transfer is in the client's best interests. That simply cannot be clearly demonstrated if potentially valid options other than transferring had not been adequately considered and either recommended or fairly discounted as appropriate.

The word 'fairly' in the last sentence is worthy of passing comment. Latterly, as firms and advisers cottoned on to the fact that file checks would often be critical because life over had not been considered, suitability reports started to make mention of life cover but summarily dismissed it as an option.

However, it would usually be clear from a cursory reading of the client file that this discounting of life cover as part of a suitable solution was only at a lip service level, very much akin to the discounting of stakeholder pensions as described later in chapter four. The report would state something like, *"We discussed the option of life cover but you told me that you did not wish to consider this."* Job done, move on. But there would either be no life cover illustrations on file, or if there were, it was clear from the date of the KFI(s) that these had usually not been shared with the client, certainly not at the time the fact find 'discussion' was claimed to have taken place. Accordingly, it was not credible to claim that the life cover option had been discussed in a way that placed the client in a position to make an informed decision about life cover as an alternative or complementary option to transferring. It is not possible to know with certainty the exact nature of any 'discussion' that did take place but I would not be surprised if it were little more than, *"Would you be interested in having more life insurance?"*, to which clients would be likely to offer the Pavlovian response, *"No."*. Ask the wrong question, you get the wrong answer!

Which takes us full circle back to where we started this chapter with the **old adage that 'insurance is sold not bought'!**

Inappropriate use of 'tools'

Let's look specifically at cashflow modelling.

Cashflow modelling – help or hindrance

'Lies, damned lies and statistics' is a phrase intended to impugn the use of statistics to support a weak position. It was popularised by Mark Twain in 1907 but he actually attributed it to the British Prime Minister Benjamin Disraeli.

Based on my experience of reviewing a large number of pension transfer advice files, I have no hesitation in adapting the saying to 'Lies, damned lies and cashflow models'.

This apparently harsh view is explained below and is firmly based on real life experience of how cash flow modelling has been used by firms in recent years, especially in relation to pension transfer advice.

Cashflow modelling assumptions

When reviewing advice on DB transfers since 2015, it was not at all uncommon to come across cases where different projections would result in the client receiving a very confusing mixed message.

Metric ...	*Suggesting ...*
• *The critical yield (CY) or Transfer Value Comparator (TVC) is very high*	• *Transfer is unlikely to be advisable*
• *Drawdown run out (DDRO) age is high*	• *... but your transferred fund will not be depleted before you die*
• *Cashflow model (CFM) is 'optimistic'*	• *... and your income will be higher than the scheme income too*

The first two metrics shown in the table, CY/TVC and DDRO, appeared on what was the TVAS (pre-October 2018) and later the Pension Transfer Report, so it is understandable that advisers might assume that these were comparable - but they are not. They measure entirely different things based on entirely different assumptions.

Cashflow modelling has been available to financial advisers for several decades. Initially a 'specialist tool' designed and/or used by advisers who presented themselves not as advisers but as financial planners (different word, same job) or life coaches, CFM use increased markedly over the past 10-15 years or so. Unfortunately, CFM was frequently used poorly.

The output of a CFM is entirely dependent on the various assumptions used and these were often inappropriate or downright misleading, in particular, the assumed growth rate(s). The output from these models tended to give an impression of the client's future financial situation that was not only more optimistic than realistic, but also confusingly different to the indications from the key metrics shown elsewhere for example the CY/TVC comparison or the key features illustration (KFI).

The FCA considered the use of CFMs more than once over a number of years and, in drawing up the new transfer advice rules that came in during 2018, they decided **against** requiring their use. On the contrary, the FCA expressed concerns about how advisers were using cash flow models - of which more later.

However, the 2018 rules did not **preclude** the use of CFMs, or other projections, provided certain conditions were met. The key conditions around growth assumptions are shown below:

- *the projection must use rates of return which reflect the investment potential of the assets in which the retail client's funds would be invested under the proposed arrangement*

- *the projection must use more cautious assumptions where appropriate*

- *when making assumptions about the rate of return under COBS 19 Annex 4A, a firm should consider consistency with other assumptions (such as inflation and exchange rates)*

- *assumptions must take account of all charges that may be incurred by the retail client as a result of the pension transfer*

- *different assumptions that produce different illustrative financial outcomes must be clearly explained to the client*

Meeting the requirements

In addition to meeting the demanding set of rules indicated above, CFMs must also satisfy the clear, fair and not misleading rule. Specifically, firms must use growth assumptions that are no less conservative than the mandated assumptions (see below) and, where other assumptions are used in addition, these must be realistic and supported by objective data (note that the past five years' fund performance does not constitute adequate objective data). Charges must be accounted for and all relevant projections should be explained clearly to the client.

The objective of the rules is to ensure that clients are given a consistent, clear, fair and accurate indication of how their finances might look in future so that they can make an informed decision as to whether to transfer or not. Yet many clients appear to have been faced with different outcomes from different projections, without adequate explanation. In relation to presenting consistent projections, the FCA has stated:

> *"It is our preference that the role played by the proposed receiving scheme is communicated to the client in the advice as consistently as possible with the KFI which will be provided to the client if a transfer was to proceed." (CP17/16)*

Let's consider the growth assumptions that are mandated in the rules for the KFIs. For pension products, the **MAXIMUM** intermediate rate is currently 5% (ignoring inflation reduction). The higher and lower rates are then simply 3% points above and below the relevant intermediate rate – thus the mandated rates are 2%, 5% and 8% respectively … but as required by the rules, **a lower rate must be used if more appropriate to the funds in question**. The provider of the KFI must consider appropriate 'objective data' in order to assess an appropriate set of rates to use. Unsurprisingly, given that they all work with broadly similar data, different KFI providers come up with growth rates broadly in the same ballpark. A typical pre-inflation growth assumption set for a 50/50 portfolio might be in the region of 0%, 3.75% and 6.75%.

It should be obvious that using the maximum growth assumptions when a lower rate is more reflective of the investment potential in the funds actually being recommended creates an over-optimistic and misleading picture of a client's financial future. Not a great basis for ensuring client understanding of the implications of transferring or making an informed decision whether to proceed.

So, the simplest way to ensure the CFM growth assumption meets all the rules is to look at the KFI. Provided that the KFI has been prepared using the correct funds, the intermediate growth rate used there (before inflation) can be taken as an appropriate gross growth assumption for the plan and funds that are to be recommended.

Yet, most of the TVAS reports and CFMs that I saw in pension transfer files simply used the 'default' maximum growth rates (2%, 5% and 8%). Worse, some CFM reports either used a higher set of assumptions or did not make clear what assumptions were being used at all!

Transfer advice and cashflow models

In addition to the general rules around growth assumptions described earlier, there are specific requirements where a cash flow model is used in relation to transfer advice. As follows:

> The requirements apply if the recommendation includes an indication of future performance; and is produced by a financial planning tool or cash flow model that uses different assumptions to those shown in the key features illustration for the proposed arrangement. There

must be an explanation to the client why different assumptions produce different illustrative financial outcomes.

A cashflow model can be used in relation to a pension transfer recommendation as long as projected outcomes at the 50th percentile are no less conservative than if the analysis had been prepared in accordance with COBS 19 Annex 4A and COBS 19 Annex 4C. See below.

COBS 19 Annex 4A (5)

Where a firm prepares a cashflow model, it must:

- produce the model in real terms in line with the CPI inflation rate in COBS 19 Annex 4C1R (4)(d)
- if the net income is being modelled) ensure that the tax bands and tax limits applied are based on reasonable assumptions
- take into account all relevant tax charges that may apply in both the ceding arrangement and the proposed arrangement; and
- include stress-testing scenarios to enable the retail client to assess more than one potential outcome.

COBS 19 Annex 4C1R (4)(d)
Check the FCA Handbook for the latest version of Annex 4C1R (4)(d).

Clear as mud perhaps but required nonetheless.

The problem is that many advisers have used cash flow models with transfer advice that did NOT reflect the specific rules described here. In all the many cases I have seen, there was no indication that the cashflow model had been prepared in compliance with COBS 19 and related annexes. In order to do so, the cashflow model tool used would need to have a mechanism to identify at outset if the model is to be used for transfer advice or not. In the absence of such a mechanism (and I'm not aware if any of the commonly used tools actually have such a mechanism) the individual setting up the input for the model would have to ensure that the assumptions entered satisfied the growth and COBS 19 assumptions described here. That would necessitate the individual concerned being familiar with the requirements. Where neither of these processes were in place, the prepared cash flow model could not be relied upon to support the suitability of the transfer advice – but it was.

Do clients understand the output from the Cash Flow Model?

Arguably not in many if not most cases, any more than the average client will understand all the implications and nuances of a TVC report (previously the TVAS) without clear, balanced and consistent explanation.

This is not just my opinion. It is public knowledge that the FCA has for years expressed concerns about the use of CFMs, specifically around assumptions and how well the client understands the output. These concerns first surfaced around 2017 and were formally published in March 2024. The FCA stated:

When they get advice, clients may receive a number of communications from firms that refer to future outcomes. Using multiple growth rates across different communications is likely to confuse clients and lead to misunderstanding if not explained.

What we found:

risk profiling tools often refer to the potential returns of the selected risk profile or the percentage fall a client may be willing to accept

key features illustrations will show projections where the pension provider has selected a rate of return which is aligned with the underlying assets

cashflow models will have their own assumed growth rates, which could be different from the above

Cashflow modelling can project a variety of outcomes, depending on the inputs and assumptions used. When used effectively, these outcomes can help clients understand how different economic circumstances could affect their retirement income. But if used incorrectly, it can create misunderstanding and unsuitable advice.

Foreseeable harm can be caused if firms:

do not consider how clients will interpret the output

project forward using returns that are unjustified and don't result in realistic outcomes

do not consider the inputs and outputs objectively

> *Each of these has a profound impact on client understanding and could have an impact on the suitability of any recommendation based on the model.*

The client may not be the only party that struggles to understand the output from CFMs which can easily comprise 30 or more pages, including 10, 15 or more different charts and graphs, based on optimistic and unrealistic assumptions, and which are not viewer friendly.

An anecdote to close this section on CFM. In 2019, I gave a presentation on CFM to a large audience of paraplanners/advisers. The content was pretty much as covered above.

Towards the end I included a few slides to show typical CFM output for discussion. One was the slide shown here. It actually shows the output from a heart rate monitor. Nobody noticed!

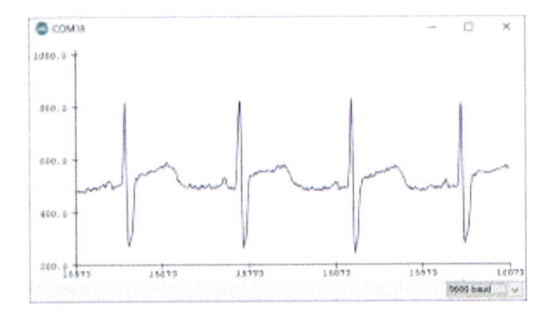

The 'safe withdrawal' problem

Another commonly misused 'tool' is the so called 'safe withdrawal rate'. Many firms advising clients to transfer to a flexible drawdown plan have placed great reliance on this outdated concept, namely that there is a safe level of withdrawal from a portfolio that will be sustainable, but did not question or test the concept sufficiently. Many advisers appear not to have adequately understood the rule's provenance nor its limitations, contrary to the requirement on firms to ensure that any tools used in assessing suitability are 'fit for purpose'. The safe withdrawal 'rule' can be considered such a tool.

One firm I know justified its use of the 4% 'rule' purely on an unsubstantiated belief that it was *"used by most financial planners and investment professionals"* and because it was *"highlighted in the CII exams"*. Taken at face value, the implication was that there is a universality of agreement with the 4% 'rule'. However, the briefest of online searching throws up many articles over the years casting doubt on the robustness of the 'rule' in light of significant differences in financial markets from those on which it was based (see below) and how it is used in practice.

The concept was based on a 'rule' that was years old, that indicated a 4% withdrawal level was somehow a safe withdrawal level from a portfolio. This is problematic in a number of ways.

First, 4% isn't necessarily safe! There is no certainty that **any** rate of withdrawal can be 'safe' in all circumstances. It ultimately depends on each individual client's situation. Even assuming that all clients are 'similar', which they never are, the 4% 'rule' has serious limitations.

Limitations
The 'rule' was created in the mid-1990s by a California based financial adviser and a number of details need to be considered.

The data on which the 'rule' was created were purely based on US assets and assumed that the portfolio is invested solely in US assets which, of course, is unlikely to be the case for UK clients. The data arose from US Treasury bond yields which were significantly higher than those applicable to fixed interest assets generally during the period 2015 on. In addition, the period from which data were sourced included a significant number of years when the nature of markets was very different to that which exists today. Stock markets were somewhat simpler and absent of many of the complex players that we see today.

The 'rule' applies only where the client's portfolio comprises an equity content of around 60% and that clearly does not apply to all clients. The appropriate asset allocation for any particular client depends on a number of factors, not least the client's risk tolerance.

The 'rule' is intended to apply where a client draws 4% of the INITIAL sum and then applies an inflation adjustment each year to THAT sum. It is not the same as drawing 4% of the (hopefully) increasing value of the client portfolio each year which is how many advisers and hence clients may have used it.

The 'rule' is recognised as being inapplicable where a client draws ad hoc sums, especially large sums, from time to time which is exactly what could apply in a large proportion of drawdown plans. The risk factor here is NOT about considering the **rate** of withdrawal but about the **profile** of withdrawal and HOW unplanned withdrawals might affect sustainability. That is why this is an explicit part of the now required transfer risk assessment in which firms must consider a number of factors, including *"whether the retail client would be likely to access funds in an arrangement with flexible benefits in an unplanned way"* (COBS 19.1.6).

Even if none of the above conditions for the rule to 'work' are breached, which is extremely unlikely, the rule is entirely timing dependent. According to research by Legal and General Investment Management, published in 2018 in an article aimed at advisers under the heading *"Is it time to retire the 4% rule?"*, for the lucky retirees who began drawing down in 1993, their capital gained 46% in real value by 2008. Begin saving a few years later in 1996 or 1997 and the capital remained static or depreciated only a little. This level of remaining capital should be enough to support another 15 years of income. But the article went on to state:

> *"However, retirees who started between 1998 and 2001 would have been much less fortunate. In the first half of their 30-year retirement journey, their portfolios would have suffered a 30-41% capital loss. The dot-com bubble and the global financial crisis have damaged the fragile starting capital.* **Where a 4% drawdown seemed like penny-pinching for the 1993 intake, it now looks like an extravagance which the investor can ill afford.**"

The moral of this tale is that, despite many advisers' reliance on this 'rule', it only works in very limited circumstances and if used as prescribed - for clients with the right risk profile investing in the right asset allocation and who, by good fortune alone as it cannot be predicted or even identified with any certainty, start drawing income at a particular point in the market cycle.

Time to retire the 4% rule? Unless firms really make the effort understand its very limited application and implement it accordingly, I think retiring the rule would be the kindest cut!

Insistent clients

This is worth a mention. The general industry approach to insistent pension transfer clients has, in my experience, contributed to at least some unsuitable transfer advice. How so?

Until October 2020, firms could charge for transfer advice on a contingent basis, i.e. where the firm was only paid if the client transferred, and most firms did charge on this basis. With the subsequent FCA reviews of firms' transfer advice and further enforcement activities through Section 166 reports, a large proportion of post-freedoms transfer advice was found to be unsuitable. FCA data show that nearly 235,000 members took advice from nearly 2,500 firms on a DB transfer between April 2015 and September 2018, on transfer values worth over £80bn in total. Over 170,000 of them then transferred, including over 9,500 who transferred against advice.

In December 2018, the FCA published key findings of its then recent work on pension transfers and found that less than 50% of the transfer advice it reviewed could be assessed as suitable.

From my own experience of reviewing transfer advice, both from that period and right up to when contingent charging was banned in October 2020, I believe that many of the unsuitable cases were a result of the following two factors:

- Firms only being paid if a client transferred. This created an obvious conflict of interest and incentive to recommend a transfer.

  AND

- The general industry wide reluctance to act for insistent clients. This meant that there have undoubtedly been cases where the suitable recommendation would have been to not transfer. Yet that case would only result in the adviser being paid if a transfer proceeded so the client was dealt with on an insistent client basis. Advisers could claim that a 'don't transfer' recommendation had been made but the client wanted to proceed regardless. But many if not most firms would not deal with insistent clients. So, an unsuitable recommendation to transfer was the poor choice made by advisers.

There were two main reasons causing firms to decide that they would not deal with insistent transfer clients.

First, PI providers increasingly took the view that they would not cover firms for insistent client transfers. That is fair enough and kind of forced firms into the position where they could not do insistent client business even if they wanted to. But it is perhaps of interest that the PI providers seemed to be relying on FOS decisions about insistent client cases where the FOS apparently found in favour of the client in so many cases. All I can say is that I personally examined over a hundred such FOS decisions a couple of years ago (it was Christmas and I had some slack time and no life!) and found that in **none** of the cases I looked at was the case actually handled according to FCA guidance on insistent clients and the 'insistent' word only crept into the client file as a mechanism for the adviser to pretend that a transfer recommendation had not been made (it had) but be paid anyway.

The other reason for not dealing with insistent clients seems to have been a degree of arrogance on the part of some firms and holier than thou 'guidance' from the PFS.

In 2018, the PFS updated its Good Practice Guide on Defined Benefit Pension Transfers (it has been further updated since). The good practice guidance it gave was pretty much a reiteration of the FCA views on the various aspects of advising on DB Transfers. As such it was a useful document.

However, the PFS also stated its view that advisers should take a blanket approach and not facilitate a transfer against their own professional advice.

> *"The Personal Finance Society is of the view that as professionals, advisers should not facilitate a transfer against their own professional advice. Those that choose to deal with 'insistent clients' are party to arranging an unsuitable solution and as such, might be deemed*

liable in the event of a future complaint in the absence of any guarantees or input from the regulator on how the Financial Ombudsman Service will interpret such claims. In the meantime, we continue to urge the government and regulator to define acceptable actions where a client's informed choice differs from the adviser's view of 'objectives: needs and wants' and introduce new rules which safeguard advisers against future mis-selling claims from 'insistent clients'."

In one sense, it was understandable that the PFS would take this position. As an 'industry body' whose guidance PFS members and others might 'rely' on, they might well fear that they themselves could become potentially liable, at least to claims of liability, in the event of future issues with insistent client business. It is also totally understandable that individual advice firms might choose not to deal with insistent clients – that is a commercial decision that each firm is perfectly entitled to make. However, both of these positions are problematic, not least because they are too simplistic and do not adequately consider the wider implications.

Deferred pension scheme members have long had the right to transfer the value of their benefits to another arrangement. The Pensions Schemes Act 2015 created additional rights (some might say temptations) for individuals to access their pension funds earlier than the scheme NRD (ignoring the possibility of early retirement being available under the scheme), and, in particular, to take the tax-free cash without having to commence pension at the same time if they transferred into a drawdown arrangement. Those are legal rights, conferred on scheme members by statute. The supposed safety net was to mandate advice where the transfer value exceeded £30k. This figure appeared to be totally arbitrary. It could be argued that the smaller the pot, the more the member is likely to be relying on the income from that pot for basic retirement income needs and probably more likely to be financially inexperienced and in need of advice. However, right or wrong, £30k is the threshold that was set.

Of course the advice safety net fails miserably where the advice provided is unsuitable but, where advice is given that meets the required standards, the result is a suitable recommendation either to transfer or to retain the scheme benefit. At this point the adviser has done a 'professional job' and has met his or her legal obligation to act in the client's best interests. All is well with the world.

But hold on a minute! What about the client who, for whatever reason, decides to transfer contrary to the adviser's recommendation to not transfer? It is important to remember that the pension pot belongs to the client. As such, the client is entitled to do as (s)he pleases with it, within the rules. Transferring as an insistent client is **not contrary** to any FCA rules. Nor is implementing such a transfer for an insistent client. The FCA long since recognised the reality that insistent clients exist and published guidance (COBS 9.5.A) on how it should be done. The guidance was based on an earlier FCA fact sheet, first published in February 2016. So there is really no issue for advisers who have a robust and compliant process for dealing with the occasional insistent client, but problems will rightly face firms that do not implement the process according to the FCA guidance – **refer to my earlier comments regarding FOS decisions.**

Firms, having given advice, are obliged to provide a Section 48 confirmation of advice letter, which is all that is required for any member to transfer their pot, so they can transfer out anyway. However, the average individual is likely to need a bit of help, not with the transfer out bit but with the transfer in bit. Access to the forms could be difficult and many providers might not deal with individuals except through advisers anyway. All of this serves to thwart the member's legal rights to transfer and, if over 55, to access his/her PCLS and/or income. That does not seem right.

However, there is undoubtedly a dilemma here. The root cause is pretty clear. There are two potentially conflicting statutes:

- The Pensions Schemes Act 2015, which confers rights on scheme members and a requirement to take advice (if TV >£30k)
AND

- The FCA COBS rules, which oblige advisers to give suitable advice and act in the client's best interests.

Further, there appear to be two contradictory FCA positions ... the client's best interests rule (COBS 2.1.1), which states, *"A firm must act honestly, fairly and professionally in accordance with the best interests of its client (the client's best interests rule)."*

... and the aforementioned guidance around insistent clients (COBS 9.5A) which clearly permits doing business on this basis where, by definition, the advice not to transfer was the adviser's **opinion** of what represented the client's best interests. COBS 9.5A specifically recognises this conflict and states that the guidance sets out how firms can comply with the best interests rule.

I use the word 'opinion' here for good reason. Transfer advice should be based around the weight given to various aspects; the critical yield or TVC, the client's view on risk, the client's objectives and needs and so on, all of which may vary from client to client. A robust recommendation to transfer or not is built on a competent adviser's view of the overall balance of these different factors. But any view or opinion is in most cases ultimately subjective. I have often seen transfer cases where there are perfectly valid reasons why one adviser could recommend a transfer and another not. It all depends on the thoroughness and skill of the adviser to pin down the client's situation and priorities in detail and the appropriateness of the weight given to each of the pros and cons of transferring. So, at least sometimes, there is no clear and unarguable case that transfer is right or wrong. And, when all is said and done, it's ultimately the client's money and the client's decision to make.

There is also a further contradiction in the position of firms that refuse to deal with insistent clients. If an adviser recommends the client's best interest is to transfer, yet the client insists that (s)he does not want to, there is no process whereby the adviser can insist on the client transferring. As there is no mechanism by which this could happen in practice, the analogy is perhaps unrealistic but you get the point. On the one hand, the client is prevented, or at least obstructed, from dealing with his/her money in a way that the law permits. On the other hand, the client is permitted to act as he/she wishes with his/her money, as the law permits. It is inconsistent.

Finally, consider what would happen if every firm refused to deal with insistent clients. Those clients would be disenfranchised from their legal rights by the actions of a group of people and firms that have no legal authority to deprive them of those rights.

Earlier I proposed that poor transfer advice was **generally caused by a combination of:**

- Insufficient knowledge of the regulatory requirements around transfer advice
- Poor objective setting, lack of lateral thinking and inappropriate use of tools
  AND
- Temptation

We have covered the first two so now to temptation!

Temptation

When talking about transfer advice, temptation comes in two guises:

- Client temptation
  AND
- Adviser temptation

Client temptation

In considering the client's temptation, we need to hark back to the start of this chapter when I banged on relentlessly around the concept of 'insurance is sold not bought' and how advisers have been primed over many years of experience to expect that clients generally need to be persuaded to buy insurance or invest their hard-earned cash not in cash.

Here is where the revelation comes in. The transfer client was and is a different kind of beast. No longer the reluctant seeker of financial advice, needing to be 'persuaded' to invest in the capital at risk assets that advisers generally recommend. The transfer client actively seeks out an adviser not only willing and able to transfer their pension and invest in whatever the adviser recommends but indeed enthusiastically keen to do so. In fact, not only keen to transfer but wondering why it needs to take so long? The sooner I can get that chunky transfer value in my own name the better.

Thus, advisers were faced with a steady flow of individuals who had substantial pots of money that they wanted to transfer and invest. And the client had to use the services of an adviser. Pinch me!

The problem arose not from the client's desire to transfer but from the adviser failing to recognise the different nature of these clients. Old habits persisted and many advisers simply took the client's wish to transfer out from a pension scheme as a green light to make it happen. The lure of the big transfer value, the option to access tax free cash from age 55, an ill-informed belief that the transfer value would last forever, a disdain for the employer or the me too scenario that 'all the other people at work are transferring out'. Whatever reasons the client presented for the desire to transfer, these were quickly and easily packaged as the adviser's basis for recommending a transfer.

What advisers needed to have done was to recognise the different nature of the client and to be a different adviser in response. An adviser who understood the relevant technicalities involved (including regulatory aspects) and was able to explain these clearly and fairly to the client. An adviser who would start with the mindset that the client would be giving up a valuable benefit if he or she transferred out so it was important to slow the client down and say, *"don't be too hasty, let's take a step back and consider this properly"*. An adviser who considered, truly objectively, the factors in favour of transferring or not and gave an appropriate weight to each of these factors in relation to the client's carefully uncovered and clarified financial needs. An adviser who would help each client to reach a properly informed decision based on a fair analysis and presentation of the options. An adviser who provided advice that was *'honestly, fairly and professionally in accordance with the best interests of the client' (COBS 2.1.1)* and who only considered a transfer to be suitable *"if it could be clearly demonstrated, on contemporary evidence, that the transfer was in the retail client's best interests." (COBS 19.1.6)*

Regrettably, many advisers failed to recognise the different nature of the relationship with transfer clients and so failed to act as indicated above. Old habits were partly to blame but adviser temptation was unarguably also a factor.

Adviser temptation

The issues arising from advisers' continuing widespread use of a contingent charging model has been made more than once already and is explored again in chapters four and five. Up until October 2020 and the ban on contingent charging, most firms operated a contingent charging model and would only be paid if a client proceeded with whatever product was recommended. In the context of this chapter, that meant the firm was only paid if the client transferred. This created a clear conflict of interest and a pretty hard to resist incentive to find reasons to recommend a transfer. That is why the suitability failings around objectives and the almost universal yet inappropriate reliance on 'flexibility and control' as reasons to transfer were so prevalent. That is why the good adviser practices described a few paragraphs ago were so often absent and poor practice was so frequently in play.

Words matter

In my experience, the most obvious example of poor practice around transfer advice was the lazy reliance on 'flexibility and control' as bog standard client objectives. Apart from the fact that these do not really fulfil the conditions to be classed as an objective – they do not describe a desired and definable outcome – they are, as has already been mentioned, Mom and apple pie. Who would be keen to have inflexibility and no control? Lazy or not, these two words were widely used in a misplaced belief that they were sufficient basis for a recommendation to transfer.

These headline words often came with a biased and misleadingly leading supporting cast of other words. The ceding scheme would be described in the negative as some flavour and combination of some, or frequently all, of the following:

- Rigid
- Inflexible
- Income cannot be varied once commenced
- Tax free cash only available if you take income at the same time
- Early retirement with penalties
- Unused fund on death is lost and cannot be passed on to your newly orphaned children

The 'penalty' word was frequently used alongside any mention of early retirement from the scheme. Its use in this context is simply wrong and misleading. First, I have never seen it described as such in any scheme documentation and nor should it be. It is an actuarial factor applied to the member's benefits in the event of early retirement to reflect that income will be paid sooner and for longer. Actuarially speaking, the lifetime value that the member will receive from the scheme is the same. No penalty!

Unsurprisingly, the words used to describe the wonderful sunlit uplands awaiting the client following a transfer out would be in complete contrast to those scheme negatives:

- Flexible benefits
- The income can be varied to suit your needs
- Tax free cash can be taken any time from age 55 without having to take income
- The unused fund on death can be left to anyone

Now, neither of these lists of features can be said to be incorrect. That is not the point. It is the connotations of the words used that creates a mismatch with the much more nuanced descriptions that would not fail the longstanding 'clear, fair and not misleading' test. The stark contrasting of heavy negatives (scheme) against the rosy picture painted of the transfer scenario is unbalanced and incomplete. Missing would be any serious consideration of the other factors such as sustainability, guarantees, charges and options to achieve the client's true objectives other than immediate transfer. These other factors were frequently where the kernel of suitability actually lay.

Many advisers failed to recognise that there were conflicts of interest and financial incentives to recommend a transfer. They needed to recognise that it might not be difficult to create a story around 'flexibility and control' that would reassure the already eager to transfer client that transferring was indeed the right course of action. But they also needed to recognise that the adviser's fundamental obligation, moral and regulatory, was to make the right recommendation and that, in many cases, transferring was not the right recommendation.

The adviser's fundamental duty of care to transfer clients, indeed to all clients, is to not recommend a course of action just because it is possible but to ensure a course of action is recommended because it's right.

It might be thought that the conflict of interest created by contingent initial charging means that unsuitable advice would be a thing of the past, relegated to that fate by the ban on contingent charging that took effect in October 2020.

Regrettably, that is not the case.

There remains a huge financial incentive and conflict of interest from the seemingly default position of signing clients up to ongoing reviews in return for very significant ongoing adviser charges.

This is explored further in chapter five but here is an extract from the FCA's PS20/6.

> *"Advisers charge a fee at the point of initial advice, but typically also receive ongoing advice charges for managing transferred funds. The level of ongoing advice charges varies, depending on the level of service a firm agrees with the consumer.*

> *Ongoing advice charges create a conflict of interest, as an adviser may have a strong monetary incentive to recommend one course of action over another.*
>
> *Over time, these charges can have a significant negative financial impact on the consumer's transferred funds and, as a result, the pension income they can take."*

Conclusion

In relation to transfer advice, it is regrettable to have to conclude that the milk is probably mostly spilt and most of the horses have already bolted. Choose your idiom.

There has been a very substantial reduction in the number of firms with permissions to advise on pension transfers. It is difficult to pin down the exact number of firms actively involved in the transfer area currently but FCA data stated that the number of active firms in the pension transfer market had declined from 2,426 firms in 2015-18 to 1,310 firms in 2018-20.

Later data indicated that around 700 firms relinquished permissions following the FCA's close focus on unsuitable transfer advice and a further 687 firms gave up permissions following the ban on contingent charging. One way or the other, as I write this, there are many fewer firms still active in the transfer advice market.

Many of the firms that gave up their transfer permissions were obliged to do so by the FCA in supervision or enforcement mode rather than it being a truly voluntary act. It is to be hoped that the firms that remain are the most skilled and compliant and that unsuitable advice will consequently reduce or disappear altogether.

And it might also be hoped that the lessons that can be learned from the pension transfer debacle of the past few years will be taken on board by advisers and applied in all other advice they provide. Those lessons include identifying genuine client specific objectives, considering all options to achieve those objectives and recommending what clients should do, even when that differs from what client wants to do. Understanding relevant regulatory requirements would be a bonus too.

Hope might spring eternal but I suspect that there will still be cases of unsuitable advice to come. Partly because some firms may still be undergoing past business reviews or Section 166 reports. Partly because problems with transfer advice or any other investment related advice can take a few years to be identified and turn into a client complaint. And partly because I would not be surprised if some of the causes of past bad advice that I have identified in this chapter still linger within some firms.

Time will tell.

CHAPTER 4 – ISSUE NUMBER TWO … SWITCHING

CHAPTER 4 – ISSUE NUMBER TWO …

… SWITCHING

Here is something that many readers have probably experienced at some point. I'm referring to the 'sharp intake of breath' from another that indicates a degree of disdain for something we have done. It might have been the plumber you hired to fix a leaky pipe who grits his teeth, draws an audible breath through gritted teeth and asks 'Who put this in for you?' Or the knowledgeable petrol head friend who, on seeing the car you have just proudly acquired, asks, 'Who sold you that?', barely hiding disbelief that you could be so easily duped into buying such a dud.

In my experience, this phenomenon seems to be rife in the adviser world too. Why do I say this? Well, having seen literally thousands of client files over the years, there is a scenario that appears time and time again. No matter what existing pension or investment that a firm's latest new client has, there is a seemingly pre-ordained conclusion that it just has to go - with an unspoken, "who sold you that" lingering in the background. And where does it have to go to? The answer is always the same, to the firm's fabulous, centralised investment proposition / preferred platform, wrapper, portfolio. Of course.

Switching can be appropriate. But only where one, or ideally both, of the following are adequately established.

- The firm can identify something problematic with the existing arrangement OR
- The firm can, with a degree of certainty, identify that the client would benefit from a different arrangement - something better

The problem is that in many, probably most, switch cases I have seen over the years neither of these are clearly established and/or not documented as even having been considered adequately.

Something problematic

Something problematic about the existing plan is often not robustly established. In fact, the features and options in the existing plan are often not even identified in sufficient detail to support an appropriate analysis and assessment of suitability. Despite this lack of detail, the existing plan is still dismissed on some very tenuous basis, often using generic standard text. A typical and frequently used example would be in relation to the plan having a 'limited fund choice'. This has also long been the standard generic conclusion for discounting the use of stakeholder pensions – i.e. "insufficient fund choice". Let's examine that further.

Stakeholder pensions started in 2001! Advisers were obliged to consider them. It took advisers approximately ten nanoseconds to come up with the 'limited fund choice' reason for not recommending a Stakeholder pension – EVER! In truth, even in 2001 it was a bit of a lame cop-out ... no client ever needed access to hundreds or thousands of funds, and the client was then usually recommended a portfolio which would typically comprise around twenty or thirty funds or to invest in only a single 'smoothed' fund such as those offered by Prudential and others anyway! So, you would think that in the intervening 23 years somebody would have come up with a more credible reason.

Here is a typical example of such a standard generic disclaimer:

"Although charges in stakeholder pension arrangements are capped, the funds available are limited. In order to create a diversified portfolio that matches your investment risk profile and provides potential for growth, access to a wide range of funds would be needed."

In isolation, when used for a particular client where that stated position has been identified as being applicable, that wording might be acceptable. But, as a standard generic piece of text, included by default in every suitability report template it is not acceptable as it cannot be known in advance which clients this would be relevant for, nor is there any robust reason to believe that a wide range of funds would either be utilised or provide better 'growth potential'.

That this use of standard disclaimers is still prevalent is unfortunately confirmed by the FCA in CP19/25 in relation to pension transfer advice that required firms to transfer to an available workplace pension (WPS):

> *"Our recent work indicates that many firms pay lip service to this requirement and recommend personal pension schemes on the basis that a WPS offers inadequate fund choices.* **Yet, in many cases, advisers are not able to articulate the need for a vast selection of funds."**

In the subsequent policy statement and related guidance around the ban on contingent charging for pension transfer advice that took effect in 2020, the FCA specifically criticised and effectively banned firms' use of standard disclaimer statements.

> *"We consider that using standard paragraphs to dismiss WPSs as a matter of course in suitability reports is unlikely to comply with our existing rules. Similarly, firms cannot simply add more paragraphs to suitability reports to dismiss WPSs under the new rules."*

AND

> *"A firm that offered a restricted range of products used a standard disclaimer in all its suitability reports to dismiss a workplace pension scheme as a possible destination for a transfer."*

AND

> *"The suitability reports included examples of the cashflow modelling and assumptions and a standard disclaimer stating: 'Please note that the actual charges may be higher or lower than this depending*

your investment choices."'

Incredibly, these lame generic disclaimers still appear in many suitability reports where pension advice, in particular switching advice, is in play. This despite the fact that the most valid reason for not using a stakeholder nowadays is that many of the non-stakeholder plans are actually less expensive than the stakeholder option.

Which just goes to show that many firms might do well to actually review their suitability letter templates from time to time and update/amend things such as this. Just saying!

Even where more detailed information on the existing plan is gathered, it is often mishandled.

Typical examples would include:

- *"Your existing funds are not a match to your risk profile."* Yet no attempt is made to assess whether the existing portfolio could be amended in order to match the risk profile.
- *"Your existing funds are not available on our platform."* So what? That does not necessarily render the existing funds unsuitable.
- *"Your existing plan does not offer flexible drawdown."* But whether and on what terms the plan could be converted to drawdown with the existing provider is not identified.

Something better

A claim of 'something better' is almost always aspirational rather than real – frequently seen is the impossible to predict suggestion that the recommended plan will benefit from better performance.

There are around nine common reasons advisers give for recommending a switch. As can be seen in the table, most of these do not usually stack up where the switch results in increased costs.

Reason	Comment
The new arrangement will reduce costs for the client with a consequent reasonable expectation of a better return over time.	If, having done an appropriate costs comparison, the overall level of charges can be reduced, it is likely, all things being equal, that the switch will produce a positive outcome for the client and the switch is likely to be suitable.

Note that all the reasons shown below must always be weighed against any increase in costs and a reasonable judgement made as to whether the 'benefit' will justify the increase in costs.

Consolidation of multiple plans into one.	If consolidation is to bring a coherent investment strategy to bear on several existing plans that have a disparate and arguably random set of investment links, then that may be a fair reason for switching, although consolidating to one of the existing plans should be considered or it may be possible to amend the current plans such that the investment strategy/asset allocation issues are resolved.
	Consolidation to 'simplify admin/paperwork' is likely to be less credible. The client's existing 'admin/paperwork is not likely to be significant and, in any case, would probably simply be replaced by a not significantly different amount of paperwork in any new arrangement – perhaps even arguably a lot more when initial disclosures/ illustrations, suitability reports etc are considered.

Existing plans do not match the client's ATR.	In this situation a switch could be justified. However, as mentioned earlier, consideration should be given to whether the risk profile of the existing plan(s) can be adjusted to resolve the mismatch. They usually can.
Existing plans do not have 'sufficient' fund choice.	As already indicated, this is unlikely to be strong reason for switching unless it can be clearly shown that the client has a need for a fund choice beyond that which is available in the existing plan. No client needs access to hundreds of funds and to use this as a reason for switching is problematic unless that need is genuine and documented. In addition, if the plan were to be switched for this reason, then a recommendation made to invest in only one or two or a limited number of funds, the reason would become embarrassingly weak and would seriously challenge the suitability of the recommendation..
Existing plans do not allow access to the funds I am recommending.	This is only a justifiable reason to switch if the funds being recommended offer some benefit that cannot be obtained similarly within the existing plan. Just because the existing funds are not funds that the firm normally uses is not sufficient reason.

| | There are many funds that any one firm does not tend to recommend that are nonetheless perfectly reasonable funds.

Many firms have a centralised investment proposition - complete with a preferred platform and model portfolios. That is fine, but it is important to remember that, just because the firm 'prefers' their standard solution, does not make it an automatic no brainer right solution for every client. Sometimes, more often than might be thought actually, what the client already has is perfectly good. |
|---|---|
| Better performance. | As mentioned earlier, it is unlikely that this would be a justifiable reason to switch, because it is not ultimately possible to predict future performance. It is certainly not possible to guarantee better performance - even if the existing plan looks to have had poor performance in recent years, it is entirely possible that it could perform better, or even excellently, in the coming years. |
| Poor performance. | This reason is (slightly) more likely to be credible but is a tall order to make stick robustly because of the 'past performance is not a reliable indicator of future results' |

	caveat. But, unlike the situation with the 'better performance' there is at least some actual data about the aspect that is being assessed. It requires sufficient research into the available fund data to make a good case that not only has the existing plan under-performed against appropriate benchmarks, **but also** that the under-performance has been consistent over a reasonable period of time **AND** that there is no reason to anticipate that the performance will change in future. The research and thought process should be fully documented.
With-Profits Plans.	With-Profits plans are not in vogue with many advisers in recent years, being considered, old fashioned, lacking in transparency and many with profits plans have had what might be interpreted as a 'poor' bonus record at times. However, when considering a switch from a With-Profits plan, it is not sufficient to simply assume that it should be switched to a more transparent, modern plan or that a switch will always be of benefit. With-Profits plans may provide a useful lower risk smoothing element to the client's portfolio.

| | If a switch is being contemplated, a proper analysis is required. Consider the following regulatory statement:

"Where an adviser has recommended a switch out of a policy because it invests in a with-profits fund, we would expect the adviser to provide analysis of the ceding with-profits fund beyond simply noting the existence (or lack) of MVA penalties, terminal bonuses and the recent reversionary bonus history."

(FSA – 2009 guidance on switches) |
|---|---|
| Existing plan does not support Facilitated Adviser Charge. | This is never likely to be a valid reason for switching.

"We expect firms to consider all of these factors and clearly demonstrate the benefits of a new investment proposition before recommending a switch out of a client's existing investment.

- *the charges of the recommended investment*
- *the performance of the investment; and*
- *the tax treatment of the investment.*

We do not consider the ability to facilitate adviser charging to be adequate justification for switching to a new, higher cost solution."
(FG 12/16 – Finalised guidance ... Assessing suitability: Replacement |

	business and central investment propositions)

There is one more reason in many suitability reports where a switch is recommended, namely that the client 'wanted' ongoing reviews but the client's existing plan can only be part of the firm's review process if it is switched. The latter is NOT a problem with the client's existing plan, it is a failing in the design of the firm's review process. There is more to say on this and the client's 'desire' for ongoing reviews in chapter five.

Switching is not the only option

Switching an existing plan can of course be in a client's best interest but, where it will result in increased costs, there has to be a clear and robust justification and the client must understand the impact of increased costs and the benefits that will be obtained in return so as to be able to make an informed decision. However, switching is not the only option and, for the switch recommendation to be safe, should only be recommended after other non-switch options have been genuinely considered and fairly discounted.

Options that should be considered include, but are not limited to:

- Amending one or more of the existing plans without switching, for example, to correct any risk mismatch or inappropriate funds or to utilise other available funds within the plan

- Amending one or more of the existing plans without switching, to provide missing features, for example, drawdown

- Considering use of one or more of the existing plans as the target arrangement to accept any other plans that it is appropriate to switch.

- If a switch is recommended in order to access benefits flexibly, considering whether that has to be done immediately or would better be deferred until flexible drawdown is actually required. The less time spent in a higher charging plan the better.

Cost and features comparison

Following initial switching guidance issued in February 2009, the Financial Services Authority (FSA) published Finalised Guidance on switching in July 2012 under the heading *"Assessing suitability: Replacement business and centralised investment propositions" (FG12/16)*. The initial guidance arose from FSA file reviews indicating that many firms were not dealing with switches adequately, leading to unsuitable advice.

Although the 2012 paper is now over 12 years old and was issued by the FCA's predecessor, it is still quoted in FCA roadshows and absolutely still reflects the current regulatory position.

I imagine that at least some readers will have seen, or heard of, the 1955 film, 'The Seven Year Itch'. The premise of the film, whose title has passed into common usage, is that relationships hit a rocky patch after seven years. In the film, the itch referred to a married man being tempted into infidelity by the obvious attractions of a blonde neighbour, played by Marilyn Monroe. This was the film with the famous scene in which Marilyn's skirt is lifted by the draught from a subway grating. Apparently, it took forty takes to get the shot as she kept fluffing her lines.

So, what does that have to do with pension switches I hear you ask? Granted, the connection is probably a little bit tenuous here. But I was first reminded of the film when I wrote an article a few years ago about switch issues, having realised that seven years had elapsed since the original guidance was issued yet I was still seeing case after case where a pension switch was recommended but where the suitability and compliance adequacy of the advice was at best open to challenge.

Arguably the most essential step in providing suitable and compliant switch advice is the requirement to undertake a costs and features comparison.

From FG12/16 …

> *"We expect firms to consider the issue of cost for all recommendations to replace a client's existing investment. … where a more expensive solution is recommended, there needs to be a good reason and this reason needs to be justified to the client.*
>
> *The most common reason for unsuitable advice identified in the … earlier pension switching review, was unnecessary additional costs. Where the advice is to switch or transfer an existing investment to a new investment, we expect to see firms conduct a cost comparison between the two solutions.* **Firms should consider all the costs associated with the existing investment and the recommended product or portfolio.**
>
> *Firms should also consider the impact of initial costs. Where additional costs apply, firms must judge whether they are suitable in light of the needs and objectives of the client.* **Additional costs may be justifiable where they are associated with a specific benefit that is valued by the client.** *Firms should disclose any difference in the cost in a way that is fair, clear and not misleading.*

The FSA found four key unsuitability outcomes that were the most likely causes of unsuitable switching advice.

Top of the list by a mile was increased costs …

> *Key unsuitable outcome 1:*
>
> *The customer has been switched to a pension that is more expensive than their existing one(s) or a stakeholder pension (because of exit penalties and/or initial costs and ongoing costs of the receiving scheme versus the old scheme or a stakeholder pension) without good reason.*

… so it was no great surprise that firms were reminded of the costs comparison requirement in COBS 9A.2.

> *When providing a personal recommendation in relation to an insurance-based investment product that involves switching between underlying investment assets a firm must also collect the necessary information on the client's existing underlying investment assets and the recommended new investment assets and* **must undertake an analysis of the expected costs and benefits of the switch, such that it is reasonably able to demonstrate that the benefits of switching are expected to be greater than the costs.**

Like for like

For a switch recommendation to be suitable, advisers must clearly demonstrate that the switch is in the client's best interest and that the advice represents value for the client. A key component in achieving this is that a *'like for like'* cost comparison is done. It is necessary to define what is meant by the phrase 'like for like'.

Like for like comparison

*I don't like your plan
I like my plan*

Over a prolonged period, way past when the rules required more, many firms merely compared the ceding plan against the proposed plan on a features, past performance and product charges basis in order to demonstrate how the **products** compared 'like for like'. It is unfortunate that the practice has not completely disappeared. Although this product only comparison might have some theoretical incidental value, it is certainly not sufficient to demonstrate suitability.

Bearing in mind the guidance stating that - *"Firms should consider **all** the costs associated with the existing investment and the recommended product or portfolio."* - like for like requires a comparison of the before and after switch **situations**, not just consideration of the **products** in isolation. This

151

means that all charges that will apply after must be included in the comparison - plan charges, fund management charges and, arguably of greatest impact, initial and ongoing adviser charges.

When considering switching more than one existing plan, a comparison must be done separately for each plan, using the intended full adviser charges against each plan, no matter how small the plan. The logic of this is that it is possible the cost comparisons could result in only one plan being suitable for switching. If that plan is switched, it will carry all the initial and ongoing charges* that have been agreed and so it is appropriate that the comparison is based on that assumption. It is not valid to assume that if one plan can be justifiably switched, all the others can too.

(* If charges are contingent, they will probably only relate to the amount actually switched under most current adviser charging models.)

So, the general rule is that the cost comparison should include **all** charges that apply to both the pre and post switch situation - with one exception … non-contingent charges. Where a client is to be charged on a non-contingent basis, such that part or all of the fee will be charged whether or not the client proceeds with the switch, then that element of the fee can either be added to both sides of the comparison … or omitted from both sides. It's neutral to the comparison arithmetic.

The seven-year itch – true or false?

Just for the record, many research projects have tried to see if there is any evidence for the seven-year itch concept. There isn't! It just is not borne out by any evidence examined by serious researchers. Perhaps not a surprise given that the film was based around the fictional theory of a fictional psychologist. Furthermore, the original title of the book on which the film was based was the ten-year itch. The author only changed it because he thought that seven-year itch had a better ring to it!

However, while the seven-year itch may not be true, it is undoubtedly true that firms need to deal with switch advice better, first time, every time, and not need forty takes to get it right!

Otherwise, client complaints and the Financial Ombudsman Service (FOS) await.

Why do switches fail at the FOS?

Replacement business continues to carry a high propensity for unsuitable advice so it is important that switches are recommended according to the standards required. That there is a problem to be addressed is confirmed regularly by published FOS decisions.

Clearly there will be a variety of reasons why complaints are upheld by the FOS. Nonetheless, a quick trawl through a few cases does indicate that the primary reason is that the switch resulted in an increase in costs. This does not automatically render a switch unsuitable as the switch might bring with it a number of other benefits that justify the cost increase. However, there are two main problems with many switches. The first is that the perceived benefits are often not obviously tangible, nor substantial enough to warrant the additional costs incurred.

The second problem is of even greater concern – namely that the cost comparison required by COBS rules was either done incorrectly, not done at all or, if done, it did not present the client with a clear indication that costs would increase, or the impact that the additional ongoing costs could have on future returns. In many cases, firms continue to compare the costs of Plan A with Plan B, resolutely refusing to recognise that the rules require the comparison to take account of **all** charges that will apply, including initial and ongoing adviser charges. Here are a few quotes from published FOS decisions. SIPP refers to Self Invested Pension Plan.

"Miss W also received a switching report as part of the advice to transfer her pension plan. This compared her existing pension plan against what could be achieved if it was transferred to the new provider. This comparison didn't however include the 1% charge for ongoing advice. The adjudicator that looked into the complaint thought it should be upheld as he didn't think the charges had been sufficiently disclosed. He also said that as the ongoing advice charge wasn't included in the switching report, Miss W wasn't able to

make an informed decision on whether the transfer was in her best interest."

"The firm stated that the SIPP was suitable for Mrs C as it had lower charges than the personal pension. Although the SIPP had a 0.5% annual management charge, there were other charges associated with the transaction. There was a 5% initial charge, 1% ongoing charge and charges against the underlying funds. I'm satisfied the overall charges for the SIPP were higher than Mrs C's original pension."

"The cost comparison the firm provided to Mr A was misleading when it stated that the SIPP needed to generate a return of 0.19% per year more than his personal pension in order to produce the same return – our adjudicator noted this comparison failed to take into account both the 3.50% initial adviser charge and 1.00% annual adviser charge associated with the switch into the SIPP."

And also …

As mentioned earlier, often running alongside a missing or non-compliant costs comparison is the failure to consider whether 'issues' with the client's existing plan can be addressed without incurring the extra costs of switching. They often can be. Here is a quote from one FOS decision relating to the commonly seen twins – *'your existing plan does not match your risk profile'* and *'your existing plan has limited fund choice'.*

"The firm assessed Ms C as having a "highest medium" attitude to risk and said the fund she was invested in wasn't consistent with this. But there would of course have been other alternative funds to which Ms C could have switched within the Scottish Widows plan if indeed her risk appetite was greater. I'm not persuaded that Ms C would have wanted or needed a particularly extensive or exotic array of funds or investments which could only have been accessed through a SIPP. Her other assets and circumstances suggest to me that the range offered by a well-established provider such as Scottish Widows should have sufficed for her purposes. And if Ms C had needed an annual review to monitor whether the chosen fund (or funds) remained suitable, then this could have been achieved without the need to transfer to the SIPP."

It is worth noting in passing that the last sentence of this quote also relates to the *'client wanted / needed ongoing review'* proposition mentioned earlier and covered in greater detail in chapter five. It also hints at the *'your existing plan cannot facilitate adviser charging'* rationale. As already mentioned, this is never a robust justification for a switch.

Default switching – the real problem

Okay, so there are continuing compliance and suitability issues around a lot of switch advice. The rules are clear and firms that cannot muster a good fact find followed by a well-researched and presented recommendation to switch only where objectively justified really deserve whatever adverse consequences arise later. But affected clients do not deserve the adverse consequences of unsuitable advice.

The suitability and compliance failings indicated in this chapter can and should be readily addressed. The more fundamental problem is that firms have a very obvious built-in incentive to switch a client's existing plans. This arises from the existence of 'preferred' solutions and investment propositions. And the 'problem' with the client's existing plan often boils down to little more than *'it's not in our preferred model portfolio'*. The firm's preferred solution is often more expensive, especially when new ongoing charges are included, leading to the difficulty of defending future complaints that is clearly demonstrated in the FOS decisions quoted earlier.

Regardless of any cost comparisons and analysis of the existing plans indicating either more or less robust grounds for switching, experience strongly suggests, to me at least, that the primary driver for many switches is that a majority of firms appear to have a default position around the provision of ongoing reviews to most or all clients. Client detriment issues almost certainly exist as a result. This is examined in further in chapter five.

However, even clients who genuinely need or want to have ongoing reviews may well have arrived at the firm with existing plans that, by any objective analysis, are perfectly suitable for the client's needs and, if analysed objectively and fairly, do not merit being switched to another, often more expensive, arrangement. The reason that they are switched is because the firms' ongoing review processes are almost always built entirely around the use of a preferred platform / investment proposition with no consideration of how to incorporate 'non-preferred' but perfectly appropriate existing arrangements within the review process.

Now, I am quite certain that, other than this fundamental omission of 'third-party' plans from the review process, most firms will have taken some time and care to research and select a preferred investment proposition. It will be reviewed from time to time by each firm's investment committee and presumably each firm will have a high degree of confidence that the chosen solution is a good solution for its clients. Fair enough, but firms need to recognise that, no matter how robustly created, that solution is just that firm's preferred solution. Other adviser firms will equally have undergone the same process and come up with a different preference. Firm A prefers its solutions …firm B prefers its different solutions! Both should be considered valid client solutions. Regardless of how much belief the firm has in its preferred solution, it is not appropriate to advise the client from a narrow mindset that concludes that what is wrong with a client's existing plan(s) is merely that they are not in the firm's standard proposition.

As mentioned earlier, omitting from the review process any means by which 'third-party' plans can be part of ongoing discussions is not a problem with the client's existing plan(s) but a weakness in the firm's review process. To stretch a restaurant analogy, it is obviously easier for firms to squeeze clients into their standard fixed menu rather than bother with daily board specials or diners' dietary requirements. It is also easier for the firm to simply have ongoing adviser charges facilitated by their familiar preferred platform rather than have to administer a separate charge being facilitated by a third party or, God forbid, having to charge the client directly! Shoehorning all existing plans into the firm's preferred proposition and relying on provider facilitated adviser charges may well be easier for the firm? But good advice is supposed to be driven by what is best for the client not what is easier for the firm. So let's talk about shoehorning.

Shoehorning

As already mentioned, most firms have created some form of preferred investment solution. The finalised guidance paper, FG12/16, referred to these as Centralised Investment Propositions (CIP), and defined a CIP as "reflecting a standardised approach to providing investment advice".

Examples include:

- **Portfolio advice services** – *recommending a portfolio of investments that is designed to meet a target asset allocation. Firms may operate a number of these 'model* *portfolios' to meet the needs and objectives of clients with different risk profiles.*

- **Discretionary investment management** – *either in-house or referred to a third party where the adviser has some say in the investment strategy adopted.*
- **Distributor-influenced funds (DIFs).**

While the regulator acknowledged that a well thought out CIP could be beneficial for some clients, the paper stated that firms should remember that CIPs are not suitable for all clients

The thematic review found evidence of 'shoehorning'.

- Some firms operated a CIP as the ***automatic*** investment solution for all clients.
- Firms did not always ensure that advisers were competent to identify when the CIP was ***not*** a suitable investment solution for a client. This resulted in advisers recommending the CIP to clients for whom it was not suitable.

As indicated in this chapter, the first of these issues, namely the default switching of new clients' existing plans, does appear to persist to this day. In my experience, the second issue is not an individual adviser problem but one of design/selection of the preferred investment solution. Under PROD and Consumer Duty rules, firms should identify not only the type of client (target market) for whom their preferred solution is potentially suitable but also those clients for whom it is not considered suitable and where a bespoke or different solution should be recommended. The latter does not appear to be identified clearly enough or at all in many firms so helping to perpetuate the default switching habit. This target market segmentation was not explicit prior to PROD rules but surely should have formed part of any comprehensive consideration of a firm's CIP.

Unfortunately, this default switching mind set is arguably an even greater risk to clients when done 'in bulk'. Consolidator firms, or firms that acquire a few client banks or retiring adviser firms, also usually have a CIP of some description.

In chapter five, I refer to the conventional business wisdom and desirability of building repeat customers and recurring income but point out that this conventional business strategy doesn't sit comfortably for regulated adviser firms as it creates a conflict with several compliance requirements that apply to a regulated adviser business.

Similarly, it can be good business strategy to aim for business growth. Acquiring smaller firms is one of the ways that is often achieved. Acquisitions tend to work best when 'economies of scale' and streamlining of business processes can be achieved – for example, removing or merging duplicated functions such as HR or bringing the acquired firm's processes in line with those operated by the acquiring firm. That is all classic business school stuff. But, as with the recurring income situation described in chapter five, the streamlining of processes in regulated acquisition/consolidation scenarios undoubtedly brings with it the risk of shoehorning the acquired clients through a factory line type process into the acquirer's preferred investment solutions, regardless of whether those solutions are better or worse than those the clients are already in, or whether the 'new' solution is suitable for a particular individual client.

The risk of conflict of interest and client detriment is further exacerbated where the acquiring firm's CIP is effectively an 'in-house' solution, perhaps discretionary managed portfolios offered via a subsidiary or otherwise related firm and providing an additional layer of fees to the firm.

Despite the rules around conflicts of interest Consumer Duty, this shoehorning situation is certainly not hypothetical. I have been aware of more than one example of firms' practice/policy that would appear to constitute shoehorning. One potential example in the public domain was reported on Citywire on 26 September 2024 under the headline and sub-head:

> *"TWP tells advisers to use MPS backed by shared PE investor*

A new edict by the management of IWP that its advisers use one MPS has raised questions about the conflicts and influence of private equity on the advice market."

The article included email wording that it is alleged was shared with advisers and paraplanners at IWP.

> **IWP email**
>
> You will have seen an update this morning, regarding the new annual review process and the collateral now available.
>
> This is a mandatory process change that takes effect immediately. Moving forward, our advisers are required to recommend Square Mile for all suitable clients during their annual review to ensure we continue with providing best advice.
>
> For those responsible for drafting the annual review suitability letters, please make sure that advisers are recommending this switch from today's meetings onwards (all inserts are now available), and that the file notes you receive reflect this change. Note that there is no option to remain with an alternative MPS solution, as the exceptions process will not accommodate cases based on cost or performance.
>
> Your cooperation in implementing this change is essential, and I appreciate your continued commitment and support.

It is noteworthy that the email appears to qualify the edict by stating it is limited to 'suitable clients' - *"advisers are* *required to recommend Square Mile for all **suitable** clients"* ... yet contradicts this with the later statement ...

*"Note that there is no option to remain with an alternative MPS solution, as **the exceptions process will not accommodate cases based on cost or performance.**"*

This would not appear to comply with the regulator's 2012 guidance on replacement business. As already indicated, this guidance remains valid. And, in its February 2017 paper, *"Supervision review report: Acquiring clients from other firms",* aimed specifically at acquirers and consolidators, the FCA reaffirmed the requirement to undertake a cost comparison.

Suitability of replacement business

To ensure it is acting in the client's best interests, where a firm's advice is to switch or transfer an existing investment to a new investment, we expect it to carry out a cost comparison between the two solutions. One cost a client may incur is a contingent initial adviser charge, levied if the client goes ahead with the new recommendation. Some of the firm client files we reviewed raised concern that firms may not always be considering the impact of contingent initial adviser charges on the future value of client investments. We expect all relevant costs incurred by the client to be considered in determining the suitability of the recommendation to switch or transfer investment business (see COBS 6.1A.16G).

> *Other relevant information*
> *We published FG12/16 'Assessing suitability: Replacement business and centralised investment propositions' in July 2012. We have not repeated all that guidance in this report. However the guidance remains valid and relevant for firms which are recommending clients switch or transfer their investments post-acquisition.*

And of course a switch should only be recommended where the analysis of the expected costs and benefits of the switch enables the firm to *'demonstrate that the benefits of switching are expected to be greater than the costs'*.

Conclusion

Based on experience of reviewing many switch cases, I have to conclude that many switches have been recommended and implemented by firms over the past decade or so that do not satisfy the compliance and suitability requirements around replacement business. And I have seen sufficient evidence that the quality of switching advice has not universally improved since the regulator's initial findings and guidance in 2009 and 2012. That switching is effectively a default course of action in so many firms means that the pace of switching has not abated either. If anything, it is more prevalent now than it ever was.

Inappropriate switching is concerning when done on a client by client basis but of even greater concern in the context of acquiring firms effectively switching en masse. As with the ongoing advice issues highlighted in chapter five, there are conflicts of interest and foreseeable harm risks for firms and financial detriment issues for clients.

That the FCA is very much alive to 'consolidator' issues is clear from the Dear CEO letter dated 7 October 2024.

> *"There has been an increase in the acquisition of firms or their assets over the last 2 years. While industry consolidation can provide benefits, various types of harm can occur where this is not done in a prudent manner with effective controls to promote good outcomes."*

Firms that operate what is effectively a default switching policy, whether intentional or otherwise, will inevitably recommend some clients to switch when that is unnecessary and unsuitable.

It is hard to argue that the controls in such firms are 'effective' or 'promote good outcomes'.

The FCA has clearly flagged that they plan to do further work around consolidation. It would be naïve to believe that the regulator will not consider how firms deal with acquired clients' existing arrangements.

This is an issue that is not going away!

Action

- review how switch advice works in the firm and ensure the process complies with the requirements, including like for like cost comparison and consideration of non-switch options
- recognise where there is nothing wrong with a client's existing plan – if it ain't broke, don't switch it, if it is broke, explore whether it can be fixed without switching
- switching should not be a prerequisite for providing ongoing service where that is appropriate
- design a means by which the firm's review process can readily incorporate 'third-party' arrangements – some tweaking of the firm's charging model may be necessary
- take the shoehorning and conflicts issues seriously and act accordingly

These actions should result in suitable and compliant switch advice, remove bias and conflict of interest and create a more comprehensive and capable review process.

CHAPTER 5 - ISSUE NUMBER ONE …ONGOING ADVICE

CHAPTER 5 - ISSUE NUMBER ONE ...

... ONGOING ADVICE

And so we finally come to what is, in my view, the number one client facing issue in the advice sector at this time, namely ongoing advice and value for money. It is no exaggeration to say that this is potentially an existential risk for firms yet there seems to have been little or no real recognition by adviser firms generally of there being an issue that requires attention.

The Retail Distribution Review (RDR) was implemented at the end of December 2012. Its stated intention was to:

> *"... make clear how much consumers pay for financial advice, what they pay for, and improve professional standards by introducing a minimum level of qualification for all investment advisers ..."*

The ban on commission for investment products was based on the view that there were *"potential conflicts of interest created by commission, due to the risk of bias, or a perception of it"*.

It is clear from the published RDR outcomes that the benefit to clients the commission ban was intended to bring was an overall reduction in the cost of advice and investment products. So, it should have been obvious to anyone looking beyond the end of their nose that the FCA has ever since been relentlessly increasing its focus on value for money in the investment distribution chain. Much too cautiously in my opinion, but doggedly and steadily nonetheless.

The first explicit thrust of focus was on the asset management end of the chain, with new rules arising from the FCA's Asset Management Market Study taking effect from September 2019. These rules required asset managers to undertake an annual value assessment of each fund. The phrase 'value for money' was nowhere to be found in those rules – apparently the industry didn't like the term so the FCA agreed to drop the 'for money' bit. But make no mistake, value for money, the end client's money, was what it was all about. And it worked! Since then, many funds have been closed or merged with others, quietly or otherwise. Others remain in place but with a published unflattering report card and/or reductions in charges in an attempt to rectify the value concern.

At the same time, the FCA flagged that value for money in the advice link of the investment chain was an intended future focus. Research carried out for the FCA indicated that around a third of clients did not feel that financial advice received had been value for money. While that might suggest that two thirds were happy with the value of advice, it does not necessarily follow. The reality is that clients do not generally shop around for advisers and, in any case, it was and remains nigh on impossible for clients to compare advisers' fee scales since few firms publish these on their website.

Which? published an article around adviser fees in October 2024. Reference to the websites of the top twenty firms in the FT Adviser Top 100 Advisers 2022 list, showed that fifteen of them made no mention of fees. In the few cases where there was mention of adviser charges, the presentation of the information was not comparable and in some cases was incomplete.

The Which? finding was consistent with what the FCA had found seven years earlier. In its 2017 Sector Views paper, the FCA stated:

"Some advisers may not pay enough attention to value for money when they make personal recommendations to consumers. Relatively few advisers are transparent about their pricing before they sell advice. This does not incentivise advisers to compete on price and may result in limited pressure on them to reduce their charges."

It should be said that, in addressing this aspect, there is a danger of confusing price with value. The former is the cost of advice and the latter is the benefit the client receives, or perceives (s)he receives, relative to the cost of the advice. From research over the years into consumer behaviour and why/how people make 'buying decisions', value has been found to be ultimately more important to consumers than price and is therefore what firms should focus on. And remember, there is, in any case, longstanding guidance and rules requiring firms to consider whether the cost of advice is commensurate with the benefit the client will receive from taking the advice - COBS 6.1A.16 states:

> *"In order to meet its responsibilities under the client's best interests rule and Principle 6 (Customers' interests), a firm should consider whether the personal recommendation or any other related service is likely to be of value to the retail client when the total charges the retail client is likely to be required to pay are taken into account."*

Ongoing advice – sensible but problematic

The merits of ensuring personal finances and investments are in good shape and keeping them appropriate to changing circumstances are hard to argue against so there is an obvious prima facie case for ongoing advice. The questions are whether **all** clients need ongoing advice by default and **how often** that is required.

Looking at this from the adviser firm's point of view, the pre-RDR business model generally adopted by firms was to build recurring income. This made, and still makes, perfect business sense in a world where the eventual exit anticipated by most advice business owners was a sale of the business and the that the higher the recurring income (or related profit), the higher a sale price the business would command.

Yet, while the 'build recurring income' business model persists to this day, the expectation of an automatic link to sale price is no longer quite correct – potential buyers now are well aware of the likely medium to long term profit impact of Consumer Duty and related FCA focus and the difficult debt burden in firms where Private Equity is in play. This has resulted in a significant slowing of the rate of acquisitions – down 10% in 2023 according to Citywire research - as well as a negative impact on the price that buyers offer.

Notwithstanding the current more difficult outlook for firms looking to sell and exit, following RDR, the ongoing adviser charge, which in most firms pre-RDR had probably been 0.5% in trail commission terms, was for many firms increased to 0.75% or, mostly, 1% p.a. Firms would no doubt have considered that this presented even better prospects for eventual sale. But it undoubtedly worsened the prospects for many clients' long term financial situation.

Gold, Silver, Bronze

I did a lot of consultancy work with firms around the time that the RDR was implemented. In most firms, the ongoing service actually provided pre and post RDR had not changed materially or at all. So, it is of interest to look at how the pre-RDR starting point of 0.5% crept up to an almost universal 1% in the period following RDR. In my many discussions with firms at the time, it quickly became clear that most firms intended to increase ongoing adviser charge from 0.5% to 0.75% or 1%. When asked, firms gave a version of one of two reasons for increasing the rate. The first reason was along the lines of "I spoke to a few advisers at last week's *<Enter name of preferred provider>* seminar on RDR and they said they were going to charge 0.75% – 1%".

Call me picky but this 'me too' approach did not seem to be a very robust basis for a firm's charging model – nor did it incentivise healthy price competition! That this approach was indeed widespread is clearly shown in a number of subsequent FCA market studies. For example, the 2020 paper "Evaluation of the impact of the Retail Distribution Review and the Financial Advice Market Review" stated:

> *"In a well-functioning market, we would normally expect there to be a broad distribution of charges, reflecting factors like different service levels, underlying costs to advice firms, and incentives for firms to compete on price. However, our analysis found significant clustering of adviser charges. As consumers do not appear to prioritise price over service quality, this might be a response by firms to demand, reflecting a simple charging model. More than 80% of ongoing advice services had ongoing adviser charges set at only 3, round, price points … (0.5%, 0.75%, 1%)*

> *Price clustering can reflect a healthy market where competition drives advice services to specific price/quality points. However, our analysis indicates that ongoing services with a 1.0% annual adviser charge did not have noticeably different features to those charging 0.5% annually. This was also the case for one-off advice, where those services charging 3% did not have noticeably different features to those charging 2% or less. Nor were the charges explained by economies of scale, with little indication that firms with more clients, or more affluent clients, had lower adviser charges."*

In terms of the service provided to clients, many firms historically had tiered service levels and many still do. While it is to be hoped that firms have now mostly moved away from the widely adopted yet unimaginative 'Gold/Silver/Bronze' labels, the tiers always seem to entail some version of 'basic' clients getting a basic service for a basic charge and 'better' clients, generally those with more wealth, receiving an enhanced service, at an enhanced price!

However, the nub of the problem with this approach is that it essentially resulted in post-RDR adviser charges pretty much mirroring the initial and trail commission structure that had applied pre-RDR. The ubiquitous 3% initial commission plus 0.5% trail simply became 3% initial plus 0.75% or 1% ongoing adviser charge. Some firms eventually went a little bit further and tiered the initial charge on a 3%-2%-1% basis or similar in an attempt to reduce the percentage, although not the overall monetary charge, applied to clients with larger portfolios, so *partly* mitigating the 'one size fits all' problem with percentage-based fees.

In addition, this widely implemented charging model effectively continued and reaffirmed the pre-RDR position whereby advisers were only paid if there was a product sold. Firms' post-RDR 'adviser charge' almost always remains dependent upon a financial product arising out of the advice provided. The adviser charge was/is, in most firms, NOT described as, nor actually was/is, a charge for the provision of advice, <u>unlinked from a product</u>. Even in those cases where a few firms levy perhaps a fixed fee for a suitability report, the additional fee charged for implementing the recommendations is usually the greater part of the overall charge to the client and so does not appropriately reflect the proportions of work done. Putting suitable recommendations together requires significantly more time, skill and expertise, and therefore cost, than the minor admin on cost involved in implementation. All of this largely remains the case in 2024.

The reality is that other than for transfer advice, many, if not most, firms still charge on a contingent basis and that effectively means they give advice for free and the charge is really for the processing of a few product applications. In PS20/06 the FCA stated:

> *"Genuine implementation costs should be a small part of the overall costs to the consumer."*

That comment was in relation to pension transfer advice but is no less true of all advice. Other than the odd complaint about an admin error, virtually all the risk and liability for firms comes from the advice element, not from the implementation. Yet virtually all the charge is levied against the implementation.

Further evidence of this continuation of the pre-RDR mindset charging model exists in the fact that, for the most part, adviser charges are still taken 'from the product', rather than invoiced and charged to the client directly. My discussions with firms around the time of RDR and since often sought to justify this approach by stating confidently that 'clients won't write a cheque' for the adviser charge. When I enquired about the last time they had asked the client to pay directly the answer was always 'never'! The blockage in discussing fees started and ended with advisers not clients!

In fairness to adviser firms, it is worth noting that providers and, in particular, platforms have almost certainly constrained innovation and flexibility in adviser fee models as a result of system or design-based limitations on the fee models that they 'support'. For example, over the years, adviser firms have informed me that they cannot offer tiered percentage charges because their chosen platform can only deal with one percentage calculated on the client's total portfolio. This, despite the clear regulatory requirements on firms facilitating the payment of adviser charges.

COBS 6.1B.9 (2)

… a firm that offers to facilitate, directly or through a third party, the payment of adviser charges, including by means of a platform service must … offer sufficient flexibility in terms of the adviser charges it facilitates

COBS 6.1B.10

A firm should consider whether the flexibility in levels of adviser charges it offers to facilitate is sufficient so as not to unduly influence or restrict the charging structure and adviser charges that the firm providing the personal recommendation or related services can use.

In considering adviser firms' apparent continuing preference for being paid 'from the product' it is of course the case that there are several situations where it can be preferable to be paid via a provider facilitated adviser charge rather than directly - for example to avoid paying income tax on pension income withdrawals or capital gains tax on capital drawn from general investment portfolios in order to pay the adviser charge. But that is not always the case.

There are also scenarios where the client paying directly from income or other sources would be more effective, for example to maintain as much of the client portfolio as possible in a tax advantaged environment such as would apply where the client has an ISA and/or a pension account. In my experience, this is rarely considered and the default 'from the product' mechanism is generally still applied, thereby reducing the tax advantaged funds instead of reducing the client's cash savings or excess income.

The reality is that the default model of taking adviser charges on a facilitated basis from a product is always easier for the adviser but sometimes disadvantageous for the client. And it creates an ongoing mindset and incentive for advisers to focus on 'selling' a product rather than selling their expertise and advice. See chapter four on switching for how this has undoubtedly resulted in many cases of unsuitable switch advice.

Looking in a bit more detail at the tiered service levels offered by many firms shows that they often include things in the service description that are essentially meaningless.

These usually fall into two categories:

- Things that firms have to do regardless of whether a client pays or not, for example:
    - *"We will keep your personal data up to date."*

- ▪ *"Access to an adviser"*
  - ▪ *Or the impossible to monitor and implement, "Gold clients' telephone calls will be returned within two hours." In practice, if a client calls, the call is taken or returned – at least two TCF outcomes would come into play otherwise.*
- Things that are of little or no real value. For example quarterly newsletters! The cost of the review service for even the lowest service level usually means that adviser newsletters are really expensive 'publications'. It is highly unlikely that any firm would charge as little as £199 p.a. for any service level, yet at time of writing that could buy a year's subscription to the Financial Times or similar. It is probably not unreasonable to suggest that the FT content is likely to be significantly more substantial than the average adviser newsletter in both quality and quantity! And I must say that I have never seen a newsletter, whether produced by the adviser firm or bought in from a third party, with content that was likely to be of real interest, relevance or value to the average client at any price.

And while firms often include filler items such as those described above, important aspects can remain undefined. The most common of these would be a clear statement of how changes are dealt with. Is rebalance charged as new advice or included within the agreed ongoing charge. For example, what about bed and ISA? Included or separately chargeable?

The reality of tiered service levels is that there is often no substantive or justifiable difference between what is offered - but there is a price differential, in monetary terms if not percentage terms.

And the 'appropriate' service level is almost always based on the size of the client's portfolio rather than on the complexity of the client's financial advice needs. Yet there is no automatic relationship between portfolio size and client needs. Further confirmation of the continuing inappropriate focus on product rather than advice.

Ongoing advice – three fundamental issues

Drawing these various threads together, I believe that the fundamental issues with ongoing advice sit around the following three aspects.

1. **The charging model**
2. **The delivery**
3. **The default**

Let's examine each of these in turn.

1. The charging model

The advent of Consumer Duty in July 2023 included fulfilment of the FCA's previously stated intention to look at charges in the advice link of the investment chain.

Since it went live, it has catalysed a lot of focus on fair value, as well as a lot of chatter in the trade press around adviser charges.

Anecdotal evidence would appear to suggest that, more than a year on from implementing Consumer Duty, many firms may not have made any material changes to their charging structures.

According to research by Quilter, reported in July 2023, over half of advisers (55 per cent) expected fees to remain the same, while 38% expected that fees would have to increase!

And research by Royal London and the Lang Cat was reported in November 2023 which indicated that, *"Over a third of adviser firms (37%) have changed their fee structure as a result of completing the Consumer Duty fair value exercise ..."* All very positive, until you realise that suggests the majority of respondents in the research, some 63%, would appear to have made no changes.

It is not clear how safe it is to extrapolate these findings, based inevitably on a limited number of respondents, to the advice sector as a whole but they do confirm what I have seen in many firms since Consumer Duty, namely a quickly reached conclusion that their charges were of course fair value and needed no change! See further comments later regarding firms' value reviews.

The disparate response to implementing Consumer Duty may indicate a fundamental lack of understanding by firms of what Consumer Duty actually intends, effectively a repeat of the same misconception that existed around Treating Customers Fairly (TCF).

Professional Adviser (10 October 2024) reported one adviser as saying, *"Consumer Duty is affecting the ability to offer bespoke advice, because you have to give the right service at the same cost to all clients."*.

Now, in many ways, Consumer Duty is indeed an evolution of the TCF initiative introduced way back in 2006. I clearly recall many advisers at that time stating that TCF meant treating all clients the same and complaining that this was not possible. That was based on a misunderstanding of TCF yet seemed to persist despite the Financial Services Authority clearly stating, *"Treating customers fairly does not mean treating customers equally because not all individual needs are the same."* So it is a pity that advisers may be repeating the same misconception around Consumer Duty. It does require clients to receive the right service for sure. But there is no requirement around 'same cost'. The requirement relates to value not cost.

There also seems to be a fundamental misunderstanding of what comprises a 'charging model'. A survey by Schroders gave rise to this bold headline on Citywire on 18 December 2023:

> *"Advisers reject 1% fee model as most charge less than 0.75% ..."*

The tag line to the article expanded:

> *The majority of advisers are now charging 0.5-0.75% for ongoing advice, as advisers feel the FCA's consumer duty is putting pressure on the ongoing charging model."*

The survey was stated to have been carried out with only 254 advisers so, again, extrapolating that small number of responses to a conclusion about advisers generally may be a bit of a stretch.

However, setting questions of statistical significance aside, there is a more fundamental problem with the headline in that it seems to convey a misconception of what a fee model actually is. There are basically three different fee models open to advisers – time cost and fixed fee, neither of which have ever been in widespread use - and the most common model where a percentage fee is based on the value of the client's portfolio (sometimes referred to as 'ad valorem' for no particular reason other than to show off a bit of Latin).

Percentage basis **is** the model. The number before the percent sign is irrelevant - 0.5%, 0.75% or 1% are merely versions of the same fee model. So, a reduction in adviser charges from 1% to a lower number is likely to be welcomed by clients for obvious reasons and by the FCA if it was driven by a proper review leading to the new lower fee more closely reflecting the cost of delivering the service being charged for. But it is **not** a rejection of the percentage fee model and leaves in place pretty much all the same issues that the FCA has raised, in particular, how can firms justify different clients being charged more (or less) for the same service.

So, here we are, more than a decade after RDR, with the same one size fits all issues around adviser charging firmly and stubbornly in place.

Value not price

As part of the implementation of Consumer Duty, firms should have undertaken a review of their fee structure. No doubt some will have done this and applied genuinely objective self-challenge, while having some idea of the costs of delivering the firm's initial and ongoing services. Some firms may not have bothered at all, and others may have simply paid lip service to a review, starting with a view that their fees are 'fair value' and ending up at the exact same place. The FCA has stated that such reviews should be more than simply an exercise in *'justifying the price firms already charge'*.

Now, you may be starting to think that I would recommend avoiding any fee model with a percentage element but that would not be entirely correct. The percentage model has very obvious issues including those indicated here but fixed price and time-cost based models are not free from problems either. To some extent, the issues with each approach can be mitigated but probably not resolved completely.

So what charging model might be preferable? Discussions with various colleagues highlighted that there has been a steady move towards 'subscription' type charging models in many sectors in recent years. For example, people used to buy Microsoft Office and other software outright but software is often now provided on a renewable subscription basis. You never own it. Effectively, you just rent it. And the subscription model is pretty universal for streaming applications like Spotify or Netflix. But Netflix and the like charge a fixed price for the service provided - they don't charge according to the size of your television screen!

It remains the case that there is no perfect fee model that someone could not pick holes in. But, ultimately, a fair value charging model has to be related in some justifiable way to the cost of what is (or needs to be) delivered to each client, based on the advice provided and not on the products resulting from that advice.

And definitely not based on the 'size of the screen'!

In practice, a bit of lateral thinking might help to resolve the questions around firms' charging models. If firms were to adopt a model whereby the adviser charge is made for advice provided rather than for a product arising, I believe that most of the issues coming out of percentage/product-based fees would simply fade away.

Add non-contingency to the mix and the link between products and fees would finally be broken.

Free at last, free at last!

Some permutation of time cost and fixed fees thus becomes the obvious way to go.

Despite the thrust of the 'fair value' requirements in Consumer Duty, the FCA continues to claim that it is not a price regulator. That is true to the extent that the regulator does not seek, at least yet, to set prices or price caps.

But the fair value requirement is undoubtedly intended to drive changes to the fee structures in adviser firms and I doubt that the FCA anticipates that adviser fees will do anything but decrease in real terms over time as a result, contrary to the view of some adviser firms.

So yes, firms can charge what they like and how they like, but they need to be able to **justify** the amount they charge and the value it offers. This can only be done **in relation to the value of the service provided**. Another vital point to note, one that is often not recognised, is that a firm's charging model cannot be assessed for value at a universal level, in isolation from the benefit that **each** individual client will obtain for that service. A 'fair' charge for one client with a portfolio of £X will almost certainly be less, or not, fair value for another client with a smaller or a larger portfolio – this is the one size fits all problem.

Focus on this is nothing new. As indicated earlier, longstanding FCA COBS guidance states:

> *"In order to meet its responsibilities under the client's best interests rule and Principle 6 (Customers' interests), a firm should consider whether the personal recommendation or any other related service is likely to be of value to the retail client when the total charges the retail client is likely to be required to pay are taken into account."*

Note that this encompasses ALL charges payable, not just the adviser charges. Firms need to determine the cost of all services provided, otherwise it's difficult to see how firms can objectively assess and justify 'value'.

Action

- If not already done, firms should undertake a truly challenging and objective review of the firm's charging model. If the model has not changed in any respect since Consumer Duty, it is likely that it does not fulfil fair value requirements.

- The review needs to be ground up, starting with an analysis of the costs of delivering the firm's services and not merely an exercise intended to justify the existing fee structure.
- Consider how to avoid the one size fits all issue and how to tailor charges fairly to each client so as to satisfy *"… whether the personal recommendation or any other related service is likely to be of value to the retail client when the total charges the retail client is likely to be required to pay are taken into account."*
- **Relate adviser charges to advice provided and not products arising from that advice.**

2. The delivery

Pre RDR, it was not uncommon for firms' ongoing service to comprise little more than an 'offer' of a review. Client inertia often resulted in many, if not most, clients not actually receiving a review.

That changed with the advent of the adviser charging rules which prohibited ongoing charges unless there is an ongoing service.

COBS 6.1A.22

A firm must not use an adviser charge which is structured to be payable by the retail client over a period of time unless …

> *... the adviser charge is in respect of an ongoing service for the provision of personal recommendations or related services and:*
>
> *(a) the firm has disclosed that service along with the adviser charge; and*
>
> *(b) the retail client is provided with a right to cancel the ongoing service, which must be reasonable in all the circumstances, without penalty and without requiring the retail client to give any reason*

The situation changed again in January 2018 when MiFIDII introduced a requirement on firms to undertake a periodic assessment of suitability for clients where they state they will do so or where there is a mandatory requirement to do so. The rules on this are dotted around the FCA Handbook but can be summarised in plain English as follows:

- Where a firm takes an ongoing adviser charge, the firm has an ongoing relationship with the client
- Where a firm has an ongoing relationship with a client, it must undertake a periodic assessment of suitability
- Where a periodic assessment of suitability is provided, it must be done at least annually and be based on the up-to-date KYC information that is required to assess suitability

The net effect of these requirements is that where a firm signs a client up to an ongoing service:

- The service must meet defined minimum standards – namely the inclusion of an assessment of suitability
  AND
- Actually be delivered – at least annually.

That all seems pretty clear and uncontroversial.

I am aware of firms that are scrambling around for a way to keep ongoing income but for a 'service' that does not include the required annual suitability assessment. Be clear. This is not an option.

In respect of the delivery aspect, even ignoring the peculiar mysteries of MiFID and the rigours of financial services regulation, it is a longstanding general expectation in polite society that where one party contracts with another party to provide a service or product in return for agreed payment, that service or product should actually be provided! If either party does not deliver what was agreed – the service on the one hand or the payment on the other – there is a breach of contract and the innocent party can seek damages. That is surely also uncontroversial.

There are four levels of breach of contract in UK law - minor, material, fundamental and anticipatory. Failure to 'deliver services or goods as contracted' would be a fundamental breach, the most serious.

Regrettably, despite the clarity of the legal (and moral) requirement to deliver what is agreed, it seems that at least some adviser firms have failed to deliver in relation to ongoing service/reviews. This first became evident from occasional cases where the FOS required firms to refund ongoing fees because of services being misdescribed or not delivered.

More recently, in February 2024, the FCA requested information from the twenty largest firms about historical non-delivery of ongoing reviews despite clients paying for the service. This followed confirmation from St. James's Place (SJP) that the FCA had mandated the firm to undertake a Section 166 review of ongoing service and that £426m had been set aside to cover costs associated with the expected client redress. At least one other firm, Quilter, has also since announced that they too have been required to undertake a S166 review of the firm's historical ongoing reviews.

Time will tell, but I believe it is unlikely that significant non-delivery of ongoing reviews will be found to be limited to within just this cohort of the twenty largest firms. Of course, the cost of dealing with any such non-delivery won't be in the SJP £426m ballpark for most firms. Smaller firms have fewer clients, so any non-delivery of ongoing reviews will be of a lower order too.

But any redress costs will be coming out from a smaller pot too. It's all relative.

Action

- If not already done, undertake a review of the firm's past delivery of ongoing service.
- If found to be 100%, get the MI ready for when the FCA comes knocking.
- If less than 100%, sort it out – pronto.

3. The default

As described in the previous chapter, switching most, if not all, a new client's pensions and investments into the firm's preferred investment solution appears to be a 'default' course of action, implemented even when not unequivocally in the client's best interest. Committing the vast majority of clients to ongoing service invokes a sense of déjà vu, as it also appears to be a pretty much a default position in many, if not most, firms.

As mentioned earlier, most firms operate on a business model of building recurring income in the shape of ongoing adviser charge (with perhaps a little bit of old trail commission thrown in for good measure). Completely understandable. This makes sense from a conventional business management perspective. As a general rule, the most successful businesses in any field are likely to be those with a healthy proportion of repeat customers. Whether it be the car buyers who return to the same dealer that sold them previous cars or perhaps the restaurant that diners return to time and again, repeat custom is good. The reason for this is that it costs less to retain an existing customer than acquire a new one. Different studies over the years from the likes of the Harvard Business Review and others suggest a variety of numbers but all seem to agree that it probably costs at least five times more to acquire a new customer than it does to retain an existing customer.

So, the practice of adviser firms to create 'repeat custom' in the form of ongoing reviews to existing clients every year is obviously good for the business. The problem is that an adviser's ongoing review service is not the same thing as repeat custom in other types of business. The car buyers mentioned above do not sign up to a contractual commitment to buy their next car from the dealership. They come back because they like the car brand and the service from the dealership. And they come back at a time of their choosing – when they want to change their car. The regular diners do not commit to taking a table for two every Friday evening. It can reasonably be assumed that they choose to return, when they fancy a meal out, because they like the food in their chosen restaurant. In any case, they probably have more than one favourite place to eat. Fundamentally different seller/buyer relationships from the adviser ongoing service model.

My experience from many years of dealing with adviser firms strongly indicates that, in many, if not most firms, clients being signed up for ongoing reviews is effectively a default position. I do not see any evidence that clients plead with advisers to sign them up to ongoing advice and ongoing charges. Committing clients to ongoing service is generally driven by advisers not clients and is almost certainly, to some degree, a carryover from trail commission days when a mature client bank could provide a comforting 'passive income' for advisers and firms. Of course, these days, it is no longer an entirely passive income as there needs to be some service provided in return. But the principle is pretty much the same.

Now, I acknowledged earlier that ensuring a client's investments remain appropriate to changing circumstances suggests a prima facie case for ongoing advice. The question is whether **all** clients **need** ongoing advice by default and **how often** that is required.

Does the client need ongoing advice?

It has been said that the most expensive food people buy is the food they throw away because it has gone out of date or whatever. Similarly, it can be argued that the most expensive thing people buy isn't the thing that costs the most but the thing that serves little or no purpose or that they do not really need.

The latter thought is one that firms should bring to bear here. A firm's ongoing service may well be fabulous and also thoughtfully priced to be economic for the firm and also fair to clients – but that can only apply where the service in question is one that the particular client actually needs.

Make no mistake, I believe that the FCA will eventually be looking for firms to not only justify the amount charged for ongoing service and whether that service is delivered but also whether a client needed that service in the first place. The first two are easier to tackle as there is an evidence base to work from, the latter being a bit more difficult, but not impossible.

Ongoing service seems to have become a default offering across the market but COBS 9A.2.19 states:

> "... firms shall have, and be able to demonstrate, adequate policies and procedures in place to ensure that they understand the nature, features, including costs and risks of investment services and financial instruments selected for their clients and that they assess, while taking into account cost and complexity, whether equivalent investment services or financial instruments can meet their client's profile."

Even in the world of clients with a drawdown arrangement where 'accepted wisdom' may be that all such clients need ongoing advice, the FCA has stated:

"Our view is that many consumers would not benefit from ongoing advice as their circumstances are unlikely to change significantly from year to year." (PS20-06)

It follows that if a firm cannot evidence that a client is likely to benefit from ongoing advice then there is no possibility of demonstrating fair value of ongoing adviser charges for that client, regardless of how low those charges might be.

The FCA went on to suggest that ad hoc advice as and when required could be appropriate for many clients and, even where ongoing advice is needed and would add value for the consumer, firms should consider whether this should be paid by the client directly rather than from a 'product'. For example in Policy Statement PS20-06:

"Our view is that many consumers would not benefit from ongoing advice as their circumstances are unlikely to change significantly from year to year. ... Where ongoing advice is needed and would add value for the consumer, we expect firms to consider this as part of the recommendation, including the option of paying ongoing adviser

charges directly rather than via the scheme (product)."

The FCA's view that many clients do not need a regular review appears to be confirmed by Fidelity's IFA DNA Report (October 2024). This indicated that the advisers who responded only needed to make significant changes to clients' financial plans a few times during their retirement – 30% of respondents suggested between 3 and 5 times while 47% suggested only once or twice!

The average life expectancy of a 65 year old male is around 20 years, 22 years for a female (Source - ONS). Clients paying annual adviser charges over 20 plus years when, for many, changes will probably only be warranted a handful of times is clearly problematic.

If firms offered *'the option of paying ongoing adviser charges directly'*, it would remove the potential conflict of interest seen in many switch recommendations where the client's existing plan should be retained rather than switched because that is the most suitable advice but the option of the firm providing ongoing service on a third-party product that is not within their preferred investment solution has not been built into the firm's service proposition.

So, it seems reasonable to conclude that not all clients need contractual annual ongoing service, and some clients should not need ongoing advice at all – firms should have a suitable investment solution for such clients and be able to show that it is recommended when appropriate.

It is clear that the FCA has long had a focus on the ongoing service provided to clients and clear too that they consider it a potential driver for consumer harm. The regulator's recent activity around non-delivery shows that the focus is only increasing in intensity.

In a speech at an adviser conference in February 2023, the then FCA director of consumer investments, Therese Chambers, told advisers that charges should reflect value to the customer and that this was one of the *'topic areas [the FCA] will be looking at very keenly'*.

She further highlighted that the FCA's 2020 review of the RDR found that firms placed **90%** of new customers into ongoing advice and asked:

> *'Do 90% of all customers actually need a financial MOT every 12 months?'*

Let's examine this challenge.

Can you justify that the client needs an annual MOT?

Most firms operate some sort of preferred investment solution, for example model portfolios or DFM. A feature of most of these is the assumption that the client will agree to commit to the firm's ongoing review service and pay an ongoing adviser charge. In light of longstanding rules around suitability of advice, more recently reinforced by Consumer Duty requirements, this raises two questions.

- is the cost of the service commensurate with the value the client obtains from the service?
- is it *'part of the recommendation, including the option of paying ongoing adviser charges directly'*, i.e. is there any documented consideration and robust justification of whether a particular client really needs ongoing service or is it a de facto default position that all clients have ongoing reviews

The first question should be part of the 'fair value' assessment under Consumer Duty. However, the second question is more interesting at this point in the story. Having been involved with a lot of firms and hundreds of client files over many years, I cannot recall any example of the ongoing service being explicitly or robustly justified in relation to a particular client's needs. Instead, and at best, the ongoing review service tends to be pre-ordained and covered in passing by some standard generic text in the suitability report stating how important ongoing reviews are and essentially assuming that the client will play ball. A typical example might look a bit like this:

> *It is important to review your arrangements regularly to ensure they still meet your needs. We offer three levels, Gold, Silver and*

> *Bronze, details of which can be found in our initial disclosure documents already provided to you.*
>
> *You qualify for our Gold service and the ongoing fee will be x% of the value of your portfolio. The fee will be taken automatically from your investments.*

Shelf-life solutions - the no review option

So, experience tells me that firms rarely, if ever, make a robust case for a particular client committing to ongoing reviews. For reasons that will become apparent later, this is an aspect that firms would do well to incorporate in their advice process and suitability report.

However, in the event that such a personalised process did take place, it would be expected that at least some clients would best be recommended to have a 'no review' option. Remember the FCA's statements - *"many consumers would not benefit from ongoing advice as their circumstances are unlikely to change significantly from year to year"* and *"Do 90% of all customers actually need a financial MOT every 12 months?"*

The questions arising here are:

- Does your firm offer a 'no review option'?
- And, where a client signs up for ongoing advice, do you discuss whether the client would benefit by paying directly rather than via a product?

A major consideration in this respect is that the recommended solutions suitable for clients who do not need or want ongoing service almost certainly have to be different to those suitable for clients for whom ongoing service is to be provided. Given that the solutions may be different, the need or desirability for ongoing service needs to be discussed as part of the fact find process and concluded not later than the suitability report stage so that a solution with shelf-life can be recommended.

Review or 'buy and hold'?

Historically, annual reviews have usually been more to do with changes to the client's portfolio – rebalancing etc. - rather than driven by changes in the client's situation – remember the FCA believes *"many consumers would not benefit from ongoing advice as* **their circumstances are unlikely to change significantly from year to year***".* The adviser would recommend selling this and buying that, or 'rebalancing' the portfolio on risk grounds. That, together with a cup of tea (often the client's tea!), was generally what the client got in return for a not insignificant ongoing adviser charge. And the trend in recent years for firms to use discretionary portfolios, with a third party rather than the adviser doing the portfolio management bit would seem to make a case for the adviser's ongoing service to cost less each year than the non-DFM scenario. After all the adviser is doing less so should charge less – but generally doesn't!

Of course, it is obvious that material changes to a client's situation or objectives when they do occur should be a catalyst for reviewing things. But, in the absence of such changes, does every portfolio need to be tinkered with on a regular basis?

Leaving aside a debate on whether most advisers or firms really have sufficient expertise, time or access to comprehensive market and fund data to play the part of an investment manager, the question that remains is whether constant portfolio changes are even always a good investment strategy. There is some evidence to suggest that creating a portfolio and leaving it to do its thing can produce better returns in the long term than constantly turning the assets over when the costs involved are accounted for.

Various studies over many years have concluded that a 'buy and hold' strategy is often preferable to one where the portfolio has a high turnover of stocks or funds. As far back as 2011, Trustnet research found that *"Funds with high turnover underperform ... The latest FE Trustnet study has once again underlined the importance of sticking to a long-term investment strategy ... UK equity funds that have extensively changed their holdings over the past year have underperformed those that have not ... Funds in the UK All Companies, UK Smaller Companies and UK Equity Income sectors with a high turnover have returned on average 2.3 per cent less than those that have kept faith in their portfolio."*

A study by The University of Edinburgh (Adams/Lambert) looked beyond a comparison of annual turnover and returns within the same year. The logic for that approach was because the research was studying UK institutional funds with long-term liabilities (pension funds) and so the focus was on that turnover/returns relationship, but over a longer ten-year period. The study concluded that *"high dealing activity within the North American and Japanese equity portfolios of UK pension funds is generally detrimental to long-term investment performance"*.

Yet another* found that *"The evidence shows that funds with a low portfolio turnover and a high active share** tend to outperform their high-turnover counterparts on average."*
*Published in the Journal of Financial Economics in 2016.
**Active management and high portfolio turnover are not the same thing. An active manager can be active in that they have a high active share (the portion of a portfolio that differs from the constitution of the benchmark index) but at the same time relatively inactive with low turnover.

Even if some readers take issue with the above proposition that favours low turnover (tinkering), the abundance of research surely at least merits due consideration. It is notable that some of the most successful investors agree with the conclusions. One of the best-known investors in the world, Warren Buffett, is quoted as saying

"Our favourite holding period is forever."

That strategy has clearly worked for him. As of June 2024, he had a net worth of $135 billion, making him the tenth-richest person in the world. There just might be something worth copying here.

While the studies quoted here related to turnover within funds, there has to be a case for turnover within portfolios of funds also affecting returns over time. Whether portfolio changes are driven by the adviser as 'investment manager' or by a third party DFM, they may still prove counterproductive. Shades of the active versus passive debate come into play here. Historically, adviser firms (and DFMs) have appeared to favour active funds based on the firm's 'investment philosophy' – essentially an article of faith rather than evidence. Yet the preponderance of data shows that, historically, active management has not, most of the time, 'beaten the market' when charges are accounted for.

Ongoing charges – a real drag

But enough of that! I'm not attempting to 'convert' anyone on the active versus passive debate. That's not the point here. The point is to ask these three questions:

- whether firms can justify that every client currently signed up for ongoing reviews should be
- whether the adviser charges levied on those clients who clearly do need or want ongoing

reviews appropriately reflect the cost of delivering those reviews
- whether those clients really understand the negative impact of charges on the investment returns they will achieve.

I have already commented on the first two aspects, but what about the third?

In a world where expected medium to long term returns are well within single digits, a 1%, or even a 0.5%, adviser charge can represent a significant drag on the investment returns actually available to the client.

And that is on top of any fund/portfolio/platform charges that will apply – likely to add as much as another 1% if active funds are used, taking overall annual charges to around 1.5% - 2%.

The drag on returns arising from charges is significant.

In CP19/25, the FCA projected the impact of typical ongoing costs for a typical pension portfolio.

> *Total ongoing advice charges of 0.5% to 1% will reduce an average transferred pension pot of £350,000 by £145 to £290 each month in the period immediately after transferring. Similarly, ongoing product charges of 1% to 1.5% will reduce it*

> *by a further £290 to £440 each month. So the total deductions on a transfer value of £350,000 would range from £435 to £730 each month. A DB scheme with that size of transfer value might have a current income value of £1,000-£1,200 each month, so the charges represent between 44% and 61% of the current level of that value. We recognise that fluctuations in the fund value due to investment returns as well as withdrawals will change these numbers over time.*
>
> *(CP19/25)*

As can be seen, what at first sight looks like a relatively modest charge has a significant adverse impact on investment returns. Especially when the investment also has to make up a chunky initial adviser charge before it gets going at all. Of course, if firms have reduced ongoing fees post-Consumer Duty, or intend to do so, then the situation improves a little but the general principle of the drag effect remains and needs to be considered more seriously by firms and understood much more clearly by clients before they sign up to ongoing adviser charges.

One of the key elements for firms if and when they think about this aspect is to be more realistic about the returns that can reasonably expected consistently over the medium to long term. In my experience, many advisers appear to believe that their favourite funds will produce double digit investment returns on a consistent basis until the end of time!

There is probably a logical explanation for this, namely that people tend to assess the world around them based on their own individual personal history and experiences. I recall as a new adviser in the 1980s wondering how I could possibly recommend clients to invest in a bond where the guaranteed income had fallen from 12.5% over 5 years to 'just' 11%. This was in the context of my then recent relevant experience of UK inflation having been as high as 25% in the mid-1970s and UK mortgage rates having been as high as 17% just a couple of years earlier in 1979 and still at 10% in 1982. It was only when I changed the context by looking at longer term market history that I realised how narrow my 'expectation' of what constituted a realistic return had been.

Perhaps a bit of that context should be considered by today's younger advisers whose market expectations may also be rather more narrowly based on the last decade of relatively low inflation and 'decent' investment returns. Double digit returns can of course achieved, with some funds and for some of the time. But consistently? In the medium to long term? I think not. And equity level returns will not apply to most portfolios as less than top risk scale clients will invest in defensive rather than growth assets in order for the portfolio to 'match' the client's risk profile.

That expectations should more realistically be well within the single digit range is supported by objective analysis of market data. A piece published on The Motley Fool in August 2024 included the following:

> *Even when you factor in inflation, which has surged over the past few years, real returns for the S&P 500 averaged around 8.9% per year compounded. That's well above the historical average of the S&P 500, which is around 6.9%.*
>
> *Going forward, there's reason to expect a reversion to the mean instead of the continued high performance. According to Professor Jeremy Siegel, author of Stocks for the Long Run:*
>
> *"The price/earnings ratio of the market probably should be around 20, which is pretty close to where it is today," he said in a recent interview with Barron's. "As the P/E drifts upward, forward-looking returns have to be muted a bit."*
>
> *Siegel expects average inflation-adjusted returns of between 5% and 5.5% from the S&P 500 over the next 10 years.*

In its December 2020 paper, *"Evaluation of the impact of the Retail Distribution Review and the Financial Advice Market Review"* the FCA stated that, on average, adviser charges were 2.4% of the amount invested for the initial advice and 0.8% per annum for ongoing advice. The latter did not include underlying product and portfolio charges, which averaged 1.1%, but ranged from 0.4% to 2.0%. There was no evidence that higher adviser charges were balanced with lower charging portfolios and, taking into account both advice and portfolio charges, clients pay, on average, 1.9% in charges each year. The FCA concluded that *"Charges can have a significant impact on investment growth."*

Blindingly obvious but no less true for that. It seems like an understatement! If the S&P expectations indicated above prove to be even close to correct, it is easy to see that an average 1.9% ongoing charge represents a substantial reduction in the realistic long-term return actually available to the client – 1.9 % points deducted from 5.5% or even 6.9% points? As the Yanks would say, "You do the math!".

And the 'math' becomes even more concerning when you consider returns in the UK or European markets which are likely to form a material proportion of the asset allocation of a client's investment portfolio. To take just one comparison, data available online indicates that, between April 2000 and September 2024, the FTSE100 consistently and significantly underperformed the S&P 500's 6.9% compound annual growth rate over the period, coming in at just 3.7%.

Conclusion? For many clients, firms should be considering whether investment solutions with 'shelf-life' would be more suitable than solutions that would be better reserved for clients who actually need or want ongoing advice. Shelf-life solutions are those that do not need to be reviewed or rebalanced on a regular basis and should be perfectly adequate for clients whose circumstances are unlikely to change regularly or in the reasonably foreseeable future, so avoiding the need for an ongoing adviser charge. These clients can still come back for advice when they need it but do not suffer a substantial and unnecessary drag on their investment returns meantime.

While adopting this approach would undoubtedly have a negative impact on a firm's recurring income, the bigger picture is that the firm a) provides a likely better outcome for appropriate clients and b) protects the firm from future regulatory attention and cost as and when the FCA decides to turn the spotlight firmly on whether the firm should be have been charging some clients for unnecessary ongoing reviews.

But all my clients want ongoing advice …

Really? If that is true, could you evidence it if required?

That the client signed up for a default ongoing service cannot be taken in isolation as proof the client needed or wanted ongoing advice and also fully understood the adverse impact that ongoing adviser charges would have on his or her investment returns. Anecdotal evidence would suggest that many clients may not value ongoing advice even if they signed up for it. Consider the article published in FT Adviser on 15 February 2022 under the headline:

> **"Advisers struggle to get savers to come for pension reviews"**

The article reported that one of the speakers at a recent conference had stated that one of the greatest challenges faced by her advice firm was getting clients to engage and agree to regular reviews ...

> *"We invite them for review every year but very few take us up on it".*

This begs the question of whether the firm charged clients for the reviews that were not actually delivered. It also at least hints that many of these clients didn't need contractual regular ongoing advice in the first place.

Another firm empathised ...

> *"It's generally more difficult for someone who's 15/20 plus years away from their retirement age to be engaged with their pension and it may require a lighter touch service".*

This begs the question of whether such 'lighter touch' service was introduced and delivered where appropriate – and at a lighter touch cost of course. I've never seen it.

Inevitably, the article identified that other advisers suggested that if clients are not engaging it must be because the adviser was *"... not making the subject interesting enough ..."* or perhaps that the adviser had *"... just a lack of personality...".* It is notable that these comments were totally subjective opinions based on no offered evidence. Sadly, not uncommon in online comments.

Nonetheless, whatever the reason, there are some fundamental issues raised if clients are not engaging with ongoing reviews. Let's examine some of these below.

Readers will be aware of the phrase "Different strokes for different folks". It is appropriate to recognise that clients probably fall into one of a small number of 'categories'.

1. Clients who are actively investing on a regular basis or making ongoing contributions to their pension and need advice around where to invest and how to stay within the relevant allowances.
2. Clients with generally more complex financial needs, perhaps wealthy business owners with both business and personal issues, or perhaps a complicated family situation.
3. Clients who are now in decumulation, where the withdrawals are variable and unplanned and it is prudent to monitor sustainability versus portfolio value, or to manage within income or capital gains tax bands.
4. Finally, firms will have clients, perhaps a majority of the client bank, who are years away from drawing on their funds or who are

drawing on the pot at a steady and sustainable level and whose financial circumstances are very straightforward and unchanging, at least until they retire or, having retired, find their income needs have changed for some reason.

The first three of these client 'types' clearly have a prima facie need for regular contact with an adviser and may well benefit from engaging with an appropriate service level. Whether all such clients recognise that need or how enthused they are to meet regularly with an adviser is another matter entirely and this is where the skills of the adviser would come into play in terms of persuading the client of the value of ongoing advice. And of course, depending upon the firm's charging structure, the ongoing advice may not be fair value for all such clients.

However, a careful reading of these first three categories readily reveals that the need for ongoing advice should arise **from a client need** and NOT merely because ongoing reviews are provided by default under the firm's CIP and that solution does not have 'shelf-life', requiring regular tinkering! Firms commonly recommend ongoing reviews so that the client's changing circumstances can be considered or to rebalance the portfolio. But the FCA has clearly indicated that ongoing advice should not arise simply as a default but as a result of genuine consideration of several factors. This extract from FG21-03 refers:

> *"We would expect to see, among other things, consideration of:*
>
> - *whether your client needs a broad range of complex funds that require ongoing rebalancing, given their risk profile, and knowledge and experience of investing*
> - *the proposed product charges ... and how the level of charges could affect the income your client will ultimately receive*
> - *whether ongoing advice is necessary, given these points, or whether the client is likely to be better off taking ad hoc advice when needed"*

In relation to any need for rebalance, it should be remembered that multi-asset funds provide this built in and firms have increasingly been using DFM portfolios in recent years, where any required rebalancing and asset changes are included as part of the service.

Accordingly, those clients in category 4, with no imminent or obvious advice needs, might well be better served by an alternative simpler solution, and that would include solutions with shelf-life. Remember that COBS 9A.2.19 specifically requires firms to:

> *"... assess, while taking into account cost and complexity, whether equivalent investment services or financial instruments can meet their*

client's profile"

A former senior FCA specialist summarised this rule as follows:

"... if you are recommending solutions that are more expensive or more complex than something else that meets the client's needs, then this is unsuitable ..."

Now, once a client is within, say, a year or two of retirement, the need for advice becomes more imminent, obvious and likely. Yet one size fits all generic lifestyle fund strategies have not really proved to be the panacea that they once promised. A quick online search throws up lots of well-articulated criticism of why these strategies are unlikely to be right for most clients.

However, the question remains of why the advice for a bog-standard unsophisticated client with 15+ years to retirement should be anything other than a low cost, probably largely passive fund-based solution, with no contractual ongoing reviews.

So, I would suggest that firms need to challenge themselves with this question:

"Do we have clients who signed up for ongoing advice but don't appear to value it?

That at least some firms are struggling to get clients to engage with reviews begs the question of how committedly or proactively these clients actually signed up for annual reviews and ongoing adviser charges in the first place. Were ongoing reviews driven by an appropriately assessed client need or simply by the adviser's use of a preferred investment solution that assumed or required that ongoing reviews would apply?

So, the client need for ongoing advice appears to be less than universal but of course it is probable that most clients do want to be regularly appraised of how their investments are performing. The adviser of 20 or 30 years ago had no choice but to sweat for hours confirming unit holdings with each provider (especially where withdrawals or unit divisions might have occurred), checking the latest unit price and creating a manual table or spreadsheet to work out the current value of the portfolio (or delegating this tedious task to an administrator – paraplanners were pretty much unheard of back then). In our brave new technological age, none of that is necessary. Online valuations are instantly available 24/7 and the client should be able to access the information at their convenience. If a client can't do this, then he or she is on the wrong platform!

Foreseeable harm – the elephant in the room

The foregoing screed sought to shine a light on the issues around ongoing advice as a default position. The default use of ongoing reviews and ongoing adviser charging has a consequential outcome, an outcome that I believe is the biggest issue yet to hits firms, an outcome that firms need to take seriously – foreseeable harm.

Niels Bohr, the Nobel laureate in Physics and father of the atomic model, is quoted as saying, "Prediction is very difficult, especially if it's about the future!"

A related axiom states: "Predicting the future is easy – the hard bit is getting it right!"

And with those thoughts in mind, we should ponder the wisdom, or otherwise, of the Consumer Duty cross-cutting rules apparently requiring firms to be able to predict future events.

At least, that's how some might view the rule which requires firms to **'avoid causing <u>foreseeable harm</u> to retail customers'**.

What is foreseeable harm?

The FCA's finalised guidance (FG22/5) lists some examples of foreseeable harm including:

- *consumers being unable to cancel a product or service that isn't right for them anymore because the firm's processes are unclear or difficult to navigate*

- *products and services performing poorly where they have not been appropriately tested in a range of market scenarios to understand how consumers would be affected*
- *products and services causing harm because the firm's inappropriate distribution strategy leads to products and services being distributed widely to customers for whom they were not designed and whose interests they do not serve*
- *consumers incurring overly high charges on a product because they do not understand the product charging structure or how it impacts on the value of the product*
- *consumers incurring high total costs of investing such that the total charges are likely to outweigh the expected above-cash returns from the investments*
- *consumers with characteristics of vulnerability being unable to access and use a product or service properly because the customer support is not accessible to them*
- *consumers becoming victims to scams relating to their financial products for example, due to a firm's inadequate systems to detect/prevent scams or inadequate processes to design, test, tailor and monitor the effectiveness of scam warning messages presented to customers*
- *consumers finding it too difficult to switch to a better product or different provider because the process is too onerous or unclear*

That is all very helpful – to a point. But it is not too difficult to imagine that there could be an issue in the next few years on which the regulator might take the view that it was foreseeable as a matter of opinion rather than of fact, and which firms might seek to argue is also after the fact!

So, what can firms do now to identify potential sources of foreseeable harm in their products, processes or services? The immediate answer is to at least document consideration of the possibility of harm arising from any of its activities. This could well be difficult and would require firms to strongly self challenge. It is not dissimilar to the requirement that firms must identify and resolve all potential conflicts of interest. Again, not easy but it has to be done – at least if firms want to avoid being dragged over the coals by yet another advice 'scandal'.

The FCA expects all firms to collect enough information to be able to act to avoid causing foreseeable harm. However, while the information gathering and analysis should be realistically thorough, and identify as many potential issues as possible, the exercise can be approached in a proportionate manner, with remedial action being proportionate to the nature and size of the firm and its ability to address all or part of any issue found. As the FCA stated in PS22/9:

> *"Underpinning the whole of Consumer Duty is the concept of reasonableness, firms are only responsible for addressing the risk of harm when it is reasonably foreseeable at the time, considering what a firm knows, or could reasonably be expected to have known."*

Guidance under the foreseeable harm rule provides that, where a firm reasonably believes a customer understands and accepts inherent risks in a product (such as investment risk), it will not breach the rule if it fails to prevent such a risk from occurring.

However, the rules do not permit firms simply to hide behind ineffective disclosure stating that customers had accepted the risks inherent in a product or service.

At this point, you might be thinking, "So what?" The so what is that providing ongoing reviews for clients who don't need regular reviews and charging the clients for the privilege is the proverbial elephant in the room.

I hope that I have established that the FCA is increasingly focused on the potential detriment to clients who are placed into solutions that are more complex and costly than simpler, lower cost solutions that would be equally effective. In particular, where solutions are used that require ongoing reviews and adviser charges when the client's situation is unlikely to change, in the short term or ever. Clearly, where this could apply, there is the 'foreseeable harm' of unnecessary charges and their likely significant impact on the client's investment returns. Definitely harmful – and very foreseeable!

The solution is to ensure that firms have a process whereby clients are filtered appropriately according to whether they need ongoing reviews. That assessment should be individual to each client and not an automatic generic default or lip service assessment. It should involve discussion with the client. It should effectively be a personal recommendation for either regular, ad hoc or no reviews that is based on a robust assessment of the need and suitability of ongoing reviews for that client – or that ad hoc or no reviews are considered to be more appropriate. And firms need to have investment solutions with shelf-life for those clients who do not need regular ongoing review. All documented in the client's suitability report or file of course.

It is interesting that reports are now trickling out about how firms are actively 'offboarding' (what an awful word) some clients now. According to a NextWealth report, based on an online survey of two hundred financial advisers and interviews with eleven financial advice firms in October 2024, a majority of the respondents to the survey indicated that the number of clients 'offboarded' in the previous twelve months had increased. The survey output was in percentage terms. This provides no indication of actual numbers and so could prove to be pretty meaningless. Offboarding two clients in the last year compared with only one in the previous year would be a 100% increase.

The survey sample size was pretty small so it has to be open to question how appropriate it is to extrapolate the 'findings' across the entire adviser firm universe. And it must be possible that some respondents would only have a feel for the situation rather than having actual offboarding numbers to hand for the survey. This is not a critique of the survey as the findings do indicate something. It's just not clear what.

The most common reasons for offboarding clients included clients no longer requiring advice, clients not meeting requirements for providing ongoing reviews, and increased advice fees becoming unaffordable to clients. Taking the overall results at face value suggests to me that firms may simply be reacting to the recent FCA focus on non-delivery and the possibility of having to refund fees to clients. The reasons for offboarding suggest that at least some of the offboarded clients should not have been signed up to ongoing service and charges in the first place. My experience suggests that many firms have signed up a large proportion of clients for ongoing service as a default policy instead of as a result of a robustly assessed and documented client need.

Either way, now would be a good time for firms to consider reviewing the process around ongoing service for existing and new clients.

In conclusion …

For all the reasons outlined in this chapter, I strongly believe that the biggest unaddressed issue facing firms at this time is around ongoing service, with the sub-issues being:

1. The charging model
2. The delivery
3. The default

In respect of the charging model aspect ...

... I imagine the FCA anticipated/hoped that Consumer Duty requirements around fair value would result in early reductions in adviser charges in some firms. Various published surveys indicate that this has indeed occurred – in some firms. Further information requests and themed visits around firms' implementation of Consumer Duty and price/value reviews would then be likely to provide a hard evidential basis for continued regulatory pressure on firms that have not made any changes to charges or that are assessed to have not adequately reviewed/justified their charging structure. That work is already in train.

You may have noted that the premise here is that fees will generally be reduced. But what about the possibility of charges increasing? You might well ask. Some firms may well have carefully considered the services they provide to clients, what their typical client profile is and the cost of delivering those services and concluded that not only should their charges increase but that clients will happily pay those increased charges. Fair enough but I doubt whether that will fly in most firms. While individual clients may be happy with their adviser and the costs involved (although it is possible that these clients are happily in blissful ignorance of the impact of ongoing adviser charges on their investment returns), lots of evidence suggests that people generally have trust issues with financial advisers and, in particular, many feel that advice is too expensive.

A 2020 poll of more than 2,300 people conducted by Yonder for the Association of British Insurers found that 72% of people are unwilling to pay for financial advice. It also indicated that four times as many people wanted one-off financial advice (46%) instead of the traditional model of ongoing fees (12%).

Research from the Financial Services Compensation Scheme (FSCS), published in January 2023 indicated that almost two-thirds (64%) of UK adults with existing savings, investments or a mortgage had not sought regulated financial advice in the previous five years. Of those who obtained free guidance rather than regulated advice more than one in five said this was because they believed financial advice was "too expensive". And more than half (55%) of those with any financial products thought that *"paying for financial advice is for the wealthy"*.

So, there would not appear to be much room for firms to manage charges upwards with the population as a whole. Firms' current clients may well be 'happy' with the charges, or at least may not have complained so far, but clients age and eventually die and the rapidly approaching next generation could well be more like the general population that is sceptical about paying for financial advice. Especially in a rapidly changing landscape where online services with significantly lower costs such as Vanguard, Interactive Investor or Pension Bee proliferate. The direction of travel would seem to be for charges in all parts of the investment chain, including the advice link, to reduce, not increase, over time.

If the ever increasing number of lower cost D2C-platforms threatens the 'consumer access to product' part of advisers' current activities and the proposed 'targeted support' threatens the adviser's current monopoly to 'direct' a large segment of consumers with non-complex needs to appropriate pension products (note the careful avoidance of the advice or guidance words), it seems to me that sooner or later advisers will have to identify the elements of what they do currently that remains and amend their business model to provide that piece. I would suggest that piece is about advice not product and that advisers' fee structures will finally need to be linked firmly to the advice service and decoupled from products.

It is obvious that any overall reduction in charges in a firm will have an adverse impact on the revenue and consequently the profitability of the firm. This negative impact is likely to be especially difficult for firms that have achieved a high ratio of recurring income to total revenue. FCA data show that many firms have significant levels of recurring income, up to and even beyond 90% of total revenue.

Assessing what this negative impact could look like is quite tricky. Variations in starting levels of ongoing adviser charge and any reduced level post a fair value review, together with different recurring income ratios and profit margins between firms all affect the picture. But let's try.

FCA retail market data (2023) provide an indication of average total revenue and related retained profit in firms of different sizes as shown in Figure 1.

The data also covered firms with more than 50 advisers but, as these firms appeared to have average losses rather than retained profits, I have excluded them for present purposes.

Ironically, the largest firms may well have the biggest problem in relation to ongoing service.

Advisers	Average retained profit (ARP)	Average total revenue (ATR)
1	21936	220144
2 to 5	61730	721109
6 to 50	253442	3169640

Figure 1

Working from the numbers in Figure 1, and assuming that the ongoing adviser charge is reduced from 1% to

0.5%, the adverse impact on a firm's total revenue is as indicated in Figure 2, depending upon the recurring income ratio in the firm. These are only sample projections based on the stated assumptions and the actual impact of course will vary from firm to firm.

To demonstrate a range of possibilities, Figure 2 shows the impact on average total revenue for ratios of 70%, 80% and 90%. Unsurprisingly, the projected reduction in revenue is significant.

Advisers	ARP	ATR	Reduction in total revenue if adviser charge is reduced from 1% to 0.5%		
			70% recurring income	80% recurring income	90% recurring income
1	21936	220144	77050	88058	99065
2 to 5	61730	721109	252388	288444	324499
6 to 50	253442	3169640	1109374	1267856	1426338

Figure 2

However, not all firms charged 1% prior to Consumer Duty and not all will feel the need to reduce the ongoing charges by as much as 50%. Figure 3 indicates the impact of a more modest 20% reduction in ongoing adviser charge. The pre-reduction level of charge is not important here. It could be 1% reducing to 0.8% or 0.75% reducing to 0.6%, or any other permutation you care to envisage. The projected reduction in revenue remains valid as per the table.

Advisers	ARP	ATR	**Reduction** in total revenue if adviser charge is reduced by 20%		
			70% recurring income	80% recurring income	90% recurring income
1	21936	220144	30820	35223	39626
2 to 5	61730	721109	100955	115377	129800
6 to 50	253442	3169640	443750	507142	570535

Figure 3

These numbers are slightly less scary but, either way, it is self-evident that reduced ongoing adviser charges will hit firms' revenue and profit hard. And that is before making any allowance for the new ongoing costs of implementing Consumer Duty, the loss of top line revenue from any clients that the firm concludes are no longer economically viable or who are exited from or not signed up for ongoing advice and any redress for existing clients where the agreed ongoing reviews have not been delivered in the past.

Firms will have to be creative in managing costs in the business, seeking process efficiencies and so on. There may be a need to reduce staff numbers and/or remuneration levels for owners and advisers. Who knows? Each firm will be different.

And some firms might struggle to survive. This is undoubtedly a potential existential challenge to the advice sector.

It's not scaremongering, it is just arithmetic.

The charging model issues are real and the FCA is actively using the available Consumer Duty levers to nudge firms in the direction of a reviewed and probably lower charging structure through its ongoing analysis of information obtained from firms.

Turning now to the delivery aspect ...

... the FCA has, as already mentioned, started the ball rolling to identify firms that have been charging for but failing to deliver ongoing reviews at all.

It is easy to see why they have gone in on this angle with all guns blazing. Of course, it is ultimately because consumers have suffered obvious detriment as a result of the failure to deliver a service and protecting consumers is one of the FCA's three high level operational objectives.

In reality, it is a low hanging fruit – there is readily available hard evidence enabling an easy assessment of whether a firm has failed to deliver ongoing service and to enforce consequent regulatory action where appropriate as per the SJP and Quilter situations that have been made public to date.

Firms can't argue nuances of failure to deliver ongoing reviews. It is binary.

Firms can either evidence that promised reviews were delivered to clients or they can't. Slam dunk if the latter, leading to potentially substantial redress costs.

Finally, firms should consider **the default aspect.**

This is the unaddressed biggy, in my view! The proverbial elephant in the room.

Look behind you
Ongoing Financial Advisers
Elephant? What elephant?

The level of ongoing charges is in course of being addressed by the nudging of Consumer Duty. And firms that have failed to deliver promised ongoing reviews are now squarely in the firing line. But the elephant in the room is that in many if not most firms, clients being signed up to ongoing advice is effectively the default business model, intended to ramp up the desired recurring income.

The elephant has been there, sitting quietly in the corner, for a very long time but firms have apparently not seen it!

Regardless, the FCA has definitely seen it. They appear to be still at the pre-action stage of making clear that they have seen it and that they think it needs to be addressed. That they have not addressed it formally yet probably reflects that any action with firms in this regard will almost certainly involve subjective judgements on both sides about why this or that client needed regular contractual ongoing reviews. This is likely to be a much more difficult supervisory project than the easy pickings where hard evidence readily proves where firms have failed to deliver reviews, leaving no room for debate, or where a firm's poor fair value assessment conclusions on the charges levied for ongoing advice are easily challenged based on the firm's own documented value review.

The key word in the preceding paragraph is 'yet'. That this aspect has not been addressed – yet – should not be taken by firms as a sign to ignore this real issue – one that will, sooner or later, in my view, bite firms in the proverbial bum!

Here is a question for you. Do you think that if SJP had imagined three, five, ten years ago that failure to deliver reviews would be 'discovered' by the regulator and would entail costs of around half a billion pounds, it is just possible that they would have addressed the failure long ago?

Select your answer from the following options:

- Yes
- Definitely
- Without a doubt

That is the very 'opportunity' that firms have now ... namely to address the regulatory challenge that I believe will come whereby the FCA will ask firms to justify the basis on which most clients are signed up to ongoing service and charges when a large proportion of those clients could well have been served perfectly adequately, and with lower charges, by an investment vehicle with shelf-life.

Time and again, over the years, the advice sector has shown itself to suffer from inertia and to be slow to change old habits. Firms have tended to react slowly, and often somewhat begrudgingly, to compliance issues only when they explode into clear view, despite the bomb having been there all along for those who chose to see it.

In its snappily titled paper "Evaluation of the impact of the Retail Distribution Review and the Financial Advice Market Review", published in December 2020 – some **EIGHT** years after RDR was thrust upon the world - the FCA summarised its findings as follows:

"In summary, we found that, on the whole, the financial advice market is improving, albeit slowly."

Talk about damning with faint praise! Eight years of implementation and the best the sector can muster is 'improving ... slowly'.

There are many examples of this inertia, including:

- Carrying on regardless, basing often formulaic recommendations on poor fact finds and even poorer suitability reports – only to get into difficulties when client complaints and/or FCA reviews of client files lead to unpleasant and expensive regulatory attention despite countless FCA reports of themed visits and confirmation of regulatory expectations.
- Or making hay, and substantial amounts of money, from poor defined benefit pension transfer advice until, all of a sudden, firm after firm after firm is found to have provided unsuitable advice leading to huge redress costs, firms going out of business and, saddest of all, many consumers suffering substantial and often irreversible financial harm.
- And, more recently, firms' apparent widespread reviews of business models and fee structures to satisfy the requirements of Consumer Duty resulting in a few changes here and there. The plain fact is that if those changes were appropriate after Consumer Duty, the issues they attempt to resolve must have been present prior to

Consumer Duty. And if a firm has not made any changes to fee structures post-Consumer Duty, issues almost certainly remain.

The ongoing advice bomb has now well and truly exploded into clear view. The FCA issued a Dear CEO letter on 7 October 2024 to highlight the **'FCA's expectations for financial advisers and investment intermediaries'**.

The letter confirmed that the FCA's number one priority for the next two years is:

> ***Reduce and prevent serious harm*** *– with a focus on retirement income advice, <u>ongoing advice services</u>, ensuring the 'polluter pays', and consolidation.*

Note the phrase 'serious harm'. This confirms the points I am making in this chapter, which was mostly written before the CEO letter was issued.

It is not just a few firms needing to adjust their charging model for ongoing service, or a few large firms that have been caught with their pants down by charging clients for, yet failing to deliver, contracted service. Those issues are considered by the regulator to have the potential to cause 'serious harm' and are already obvious, or should be, to all. The issues are likely to apply to many firms of all sizes and types. Firms need to take care not to sit back and enjoy their customary schadenfreude arising from the FCA's known actions with SJP and the like. Instead, prudent firms will take another look at their own charging model for initial and ongoing advice and will make sure they have good management information to evidence that they deliver promised ongoing reviews.

The letter also gives fair warning that the FCA intends to *'undertake multi-firm work to review consolidation within the market'*. As highlighted earlier, there is already a change of mind set in consolidators seeking to acquire advice firms. Recurring income alone is no longer a sole factor in 'valuing' a business. Profit is much more important, as is absence of ongoing or potential compliance issues. Consolidators have rightly been cautious in recent years about acquiring firms where robust due diligence has identified a significant pension transfer book. That due diligence should now include a detailed examination of the selling firm's record in relation to ongoing reviews – what is charged and what is delivered and how will the firm justify every client that is signed up for ongoing reviews should be. So, firms that will be looking for a buyer and an optimal sale price at some point would be wise to act quickly and decisively to make sure that this aspect of the business will stand up to scrutiny not only from the regulator but also from potential buyers. The Dear CEO letter states that the FCA expects consolidators to *'Undertake adequate due diligence of the selling firm or client bank.'*

What does the letter actually say about ongoing advice?

Ongoing advice services

Our analysis shows that 90% of new clients are placed into arrangements for ongoing advice. The proportion of advice revenue from ongoing advice has also increased from 60% in 2016 to 80% in 2023. We have concerns firms may not be adequately considering the relevance and costs of these services for all clients and that some clients are being charged for services that are not delivered.

What we expect of you

You should ensure the service offered is appropriate for your clients' circumstances, that it provides fair value, and is delivered within the terms of the agreement. You should also clearly confirm the details of the ongoing service to your clients, its associated charges, and how clients can cancel the service should they wish. You should not charge clients for services that are not delivered. Firms must maintain records to ensure appropriate monitoring and demonstrate they are delivering good outcomes.

What we will do

Earlier this year we wrote to a number of firms requesting information about their delivery of ongoing advice. We aim to

> *provide a further update later this year on our findings and next steps.*

There are two key sentences here – the first is:

'We have concerns firms may not be adequately considering the relevance and costs of these services for all clients and that some clients are being charged for services that are not delivered.'

It highlights the very same three issues that I have raised in this chapter. 'Costs' refers to the charging model. The 'non-delivery' link is clear. And 'relevance' relates to firms defaulting most clients to ongoing service charges when many of those clients arguably may not actually need contractual regular ongoing advice.

The second key sentence is:

"You should not charge clients for services that are not delivered."

For years firms have regularly asked me how to deal with the client who is signed up for ongoing reviews but turns down the adviser's request for an appointment saying something like, 'I'm OK for the moment – let's leave it this year'. This might happen just once but, in many cases, this 'let's leave it' occurred over several years. Firms asked:

- How many times can the client refuse a review before there is a problem?
- Do I have to terminate the ongoing review service?
- Do I have to refund the review fee?

Before MIFID II came along with its requirement to provide an ongoing assessment of suitability at least annually to any client with whom there is an ongoing relationship, it did not seem unreasonable for firms to feel that they had fulfilled their end of the agreement, namely, they had tried to deliver the review but the client did not engage so why should they refund the fee. I had a certain amount of sympathy with that view but always told firms that where this happened more than once in a while, they had to have a policy defining how many missed reviews were acceptable before a discussion took place with the client about terminating the review service – my view was that two reviews was probably the acceptable limit.

However, post MIFID II and, more importantly, in light of the FCA's current focus on this whole area, I think that *"You should not charge clients for services that are not delivered."* could, and probably should, be taken literally, meaning that clients should not be charged for **any** year in which the review is not delivered*, no matter whether that be as a result of the firm's failure to deliver or the client saying, "let's leave it this year".

If that interpretation turns out to be true – and I believe it will – then firms will be in an admin nightmare of refunds for some clients in some years and not in other years. A nightmare indeed if the firm charges the client directly and even more so for the majority of firms that operate on the basis of adviser charges being facilitated by a provider/platform. And possible VAT implications on top? Let's not even go there.

(* I understand that at least two of the large firms contacted by the FCA about ongoing review have already amended their internal process such that a refund will be due for any year in which a review is not delivered.)

When is ongoing not ongoing?

There is one other related issue that this whole spectre of adviser charge refunds brings to mind. For the most part, although review meetings are mostly delivered annually, firms do not charge on an annual basis. Instead, the facilitated ongoing adviser charge is usually paid to the firm monthly or quarterly in advance of delivering the service to which the charge relates. This raises three thoughts.

1. Ongoing charges starting in the month immediately following the initial charge begs the question of whether the terms initial adviser charge and ongoing adviser charge are misleading. What the client is paying in the first year is not the

stated initial charge but the initial charge plus eleven months of 'ongoing' adviser charge.

2. A potential practical problem arises out of the fact that firms are effectively taking payment for a service not yet delivered. Worse, a service that might not be delivered. As we have seen, the firm might fail to deliver or the client might reject a review. It is also possible that the client could die or, less dramatically, decide to move his or her affairs to another adviser before the review is due. Is a refund/partial refund required?

3. In any event, does the firm have a clear legal entitlement to an adviser charge received before the service for which that charge is being made is actually delivered? Could/should that money be construed as client money until such time as it is able to be set against the delivery of the agreed service? And remember, most firms do not have client money permissions?

***

Well, the Solicitors Regulation Authority Accounts Rules consider such money to be client money. To paraphrase the SRA website,

"Firms can receive money in advance from clients and third parties for a range of reasons. For example, for their legal fees, based on an estimate of their likely costs or as a fixed fee ... All of these types of money are client money.

There are clear risks to your client if you bill for, and then pay into your firm's business account, money for legal work that you have not yet done or for disbursements that have not yet been incurred."

Check out the SRA website for examples of the potential risks. And the Law Society confirms,

"Some of the money that you receive from a client will be intended to cover your fees. Payments on account of costs are generally client money and must be held in a client account."

Just a thought!

It's a retainer

Experience suggests that many firms would claim that the charge is not in advance of the review service but is a retainer as they are available to the client in the months between review meetings.

Mmmmm!

Not sure that argument entirely convinces. Most clients probably do not avail themselves of adviser contact between reviews. How much of the charge is for the review and how much is for 'other' things such as 'access to adviser' or newsletters and the like? And does the ongoing service agreement actually clearly address any of the issues raised here, like refunds and so on?

Almost certainly not.

Anyway, back to the conclusion.

Just for once, it would be amazing if firms could get ahead of a major regulatory issue and not wait until the FCA comes to visit. A challenge relating to unjustifiable ongoing charges for unnecessary ongoing reviews will have to be dealt with when, in my view inevitably, the FCA comes to call, armed with the as yet unused 'foreseeable harm' tool, and draws firms' attention to the previously unnoticed elephant.

As modelled earlier, addressing the issue sooner than later could have a not insignificant impact on revenue but that could well turn out to be better than the alternative of future costly regulatory issues.

Be wise, don't wait, deal with it now.